How to Get All T
to Become Like
the Best Teachers

There are dramatic differences in the quality of teachers in every school. Every building has teachers who consistently engage students and deliver high-quality instruction. Every building also has teachers with varying ranges of ability. If all teachers could be more like the best teachers, then we would have significant improvement in every school.

In this important book, Todd Whitaker demonstrates how this can really be achieved. With inspiration, humor, and practical advice, Whitaker shares the qualities of the best teachers and how we can teach these qualities to others. He shows how the best teachers emphasize the learning relationship; focus only on what they can influence; and use effective classroom management involving filtering, proximity, redirection, and business mode. He then explains how we can coach other teachers by showing, not telling; by creating subcultures and learning experiences; and by leading the way. Finally, Whitaker describes the importance of hiring highly talented people who form new lines rather than fall in line. He provides strategies for asking the right interview questions, for choosing the right mentors, and for selecting the best hosts for student teachers.

No matter how education changes, there are always outstanding teachers making a difference. We can grow our schools by helping even more teachers become exceptional.

Todd Whitaker (@toddwhitaker) is a leading presenter in the field of education and has written 65 books including the bestseller *What Great Teachers Do Differently*. He is a former teacher, coach, principal, and professor of educational leadership.

Also Available from Routledge Eye On Education

(www.routledge.com/k-12)

What Great Teachers Do Differently, 3rd Edition: Nineteen Things That Matter Most
Todd Whitaker

What Great Principals Do Differently, 3rd Edition: Twenty Things That Matter Most
Todd Whitaker

Leading School Change, 2nd Edition: How to Overcome Resistance, Increase Buy-in, and Accomplish Your Goals
Todd Whitaker

Your First Year, 2nd Edition: How to Survive and Thrive as a New Teacher
Todd Whitaker, Katherine Whitaker, and Madeline Whitaker Good

Classroom Management from the Ground Up
Todd Whitaker, Katherine Whitaker, and Madeline Whitaker Good

Dealing with Difficult Parents, 2nd Edition
Todd Whitaker and Douglas Fiore

Dealing with Difficult Teachers, 3rd Edition
Todd Whitaker

A School Leader's Guide to Dealing with Difficult Parents
Todd Whitaker and Douglas Fiore

Invest in Your Best: 9 Strategies to Grow, Support, and Celebrate Your Most Valuable Teachers
Todd Whitaker, Connie Hamilton, Joseph Jones, and T.J. Vari

Turning It Around: Small Steps or Sweeping Changes to Create the School Your Students Deserve
Todd Whitaker and Courtney Monterecy

How to Get All Teachers to Become Like the Best Teachers

Todd Whitaker

Routledge
Taylor & Francis Group

NEW YORK AND LONDON

Designed cover image: Getty Images

First published 2025
by Routledge
605 Third Avenue, New York, NY 10158

and by Routledge
4 Park Square, Milton Park, Abingdon, Oxon, OX14 4RN

Routledge is an imprint of the Taylor & Francis Group, an informa business

Library of Congress Cataloging-in-Publication Data
Names: Whitaker, Todd, 1959- author.
Title: How to get all teachers to become like the best teachers / Todd
Whitaker.
Description: New York, NY : Routledge, 2025. | Includes bibliographical
references.
Identifiers: LCCN 2024029461 (print) | LCCN 2024029462 (ebook) | ISBN
9781032795287 (hardback) | ISBN 9781032775562 (paperback) | ISBN
9781003492535 (ebook)
Subjects: LCSH: Teacher effectiveness. | Effective teaching. |
Teacher-student relationships. | Classroom management.
Classification: LCC LB1775 .W4355 2025 (print) | LCC LB1775 (ebook) |
DDC 371.1--dc23/eng/20240716
LC record available at https://lccn.loc.gov/2024029461
LC ebook record available at https://lccn.loc.gov/2024029462

ISBN: 978-1-032-79528-7 (hbk)
ISBN: 978-1-032-77556-2 (pbk)
ISBN: 978-1-003-49253-5 (ebk)

DOI: 10.4324/9781003492535

Typeset in Palatino
by KnowledgeWorks Global Ltd.

Contents

Meet the Author. ix

**Part I Can We Really Help All Teachers Become Like
the Best Teachers?**. 1

1 First the Big Picture, Then the Real Picture 3
Changing the World, One Teacher at a Time and
All Teachers at Once 5
One Pool of Teachers 5
Attract and Retain 7

**2 The Teacher Is the Variable That Matters
the Most (By Far)** 10
The New/Old AI: Artificial Intelligence? 10
Pandemic: Virtual Teaching 11
Flexible Seating 12
Students with Trauma 13
Participation Trophies 15

**3 How Great Teachers Look at the World: Hint—You
Can Do It Too** 17
A Goal and a Wish 17
The First Day of Teaching During the Pandemic 18
The Learning Relationship: The Core of the High-Quality
Teacher 20
What's Next? 22

Part II Hiring Exceptional Teachers 23

**4 Two Core Ways to Increase Teacher Quality
in Your Setting: Let's Start with Hiring Highly
Talented Teachers**. 25

What Is Talent? 26
All We Want Is Talent 27
Checking References 28
Would You Hire Them Again? 29
The 1 to 10 Scale 30

5 **The Number One Goal in Hiring** 33
Interview Questions to Find the Best 36
Tone and Manner 38

6 **The Construction of Induction** 40
Creating a Desired Subculture 43
Induction Starts at the Interview 43
Introducing During the Interview: Classroom Visitations 44
Assigning Mentors 45
There Is Always a Welcoming Committee 46
The Cost of Getting It Wrong 47

7 **Improve *the* Pool and *Our* Pool: Student Teaching** 50
The Macro View 50
The Career Impact 52
The Micro View 53

Part III Improving the Teachers We Have 55

8 **Teaching the Teachers** 57
The Limits of Induction and Onboarding 58
Teaching Versus Telling 59
Why Don't We Teach Instead of Tell? 60
Classroom Management 61

9 **The Specificity of Teaching Classroom Management** 65
The Specifics Are the Difference Makers 66
Clip Charts: The Problem or the Solution? 66
When a Student Misbehaves 68
Adult Behavior 70
Redirect 71
Embedding Redirection 71

10 **The Power of Proximity** 73
Leaving for Lunch 74
The Best Teachers Do Not Try to 'Prove Who Is
in Charge' 75
Power Versus Influence 76
Future Versus Past 77
The Clip Chart Conclusion 78

11 **The One Best Way** 81
Everything Seems Random and Yet Nothing Is 82
Lunch Supervision 84
No Need to Out Quick 87
The Least Important Student 87

12 **Teach Me How to Filter, Please** 89
Everyone Filters 89
Filtering Is a Choice 90
How Many People Know? 91
How Was Your Holiday? 91
Greeting Students: Everyone Is a Teacher 92

13 **The Emotional Modes** 97
Background 98
The Three Modes 99
Earn Their Respect? 101
The Challenging Student 103
Clean Your Bedroom! 105
It Is Not an Event; It Is a Drumbeat 106
It Is the Teacher 106
Arguing 107
Consistency 108

Part IV   Timeless Truths and New Learnings 109

14 **The Learning Relationship** 111
Understanding Connections 112
The Poor Lecturer 112
The Large Lecture in a College Auditorium 113

Reducing Poor Lecture 114
Relationships and Learning 115

15 The Eyes (and Ears) Have It **116**
The Mutual Exchange 116
Pineapple Charts 117
Ghost Walks 117
Individual or Group Walk Throughs 117
Some Observation Supports 118
Classroom Management Visits 118
Calling Parents 119
Back-to-School/Open House Night 119
Parent Teacher Conferences 119
Recordings 119

16 Understanding High Achievers **121**
The Perfection Comparison 121
Driven by Confidence? 122
We Are Off to a Great Start! Let's Keep It Up! 122
This Has Been Great So Far 123
Evaluating High Achievers 124
Hire Good People and Get Out of Their Way 125
Blanket Monkeys 126
The Leader's Pet 127
The Informal Seating Chart 128
Balancing the Burden 128
The Gifts of the Best 129

17 The Bottom Line on How to Get to the Top **131**
The Difference Is Talent 132

References **133**

Meet the Author

Dr. Todd Whitaker has been fortunate to be able to blend his passion with his career. Recognized as a leading presenter in the field of education, his message about the importance of teaching has resonated with hundreds of thousands of educators around the world. Todd is a professor of educational leadership at the University of Missouri, and he has spent his life pursuing his love of education by researching and studying effective teachers and principals.

Prior to moving into higher education, he was a mathematics teacher and basketball coach in Missouri. Todd then served as a principal at the middle school, junior high, and high school levels. He was also a middle school coordinator in charge of staffing, curriculum, and technology for the opening of new middle schools.

One of the nation's leading authorities on staff motivation, teacher leadership, and principal effectiveness, Todd has written 65 books including the national bestseller *What Great Teachers Do Differently*. Other titles include *Shifting the Monkey, Dealing with Difficult Teachers, The 10 Minute Inservice, The Ball, What Great Principals Do Differently, Motivating & Inspiring Teachers,* and *Dealing with Difficult Parents*.

Todd is married to Beth, also a former teacher and principal, who is the coordinator of the Educational Leadership program at the University of Missouri. They are the parents of three children: Katherine, Madeline, and Harrison.

Part I

Can We Really Help All Teachers Become Like the Best Teachers?

Part 1

1

First the Big Picture, Then the Real Picture

Education is such a delightful, exhausting, rewarding, and challenging profession. The contradictions teachers and principals feel can at times seem overwhelming. Educators make a difference every day and simultaneously often feel that it is never enough. Teaching can be one of the most isolating professions and yet you are never alone. How can we make it through this tapestry of confusion and remain focused on impacting the young people we work with every day? Has anyone solved this emotional labyrinth? Is it even possible?

Well, it turns out it has been solved. Not only in your school, but in every school. Regardless of whether it is an elementary, middle level, or high school; regardless of the budget, leadership, community, or economic status of the students; regardless of whether the school setting is urban, suburban, small town, or rural; and regardless of whether a school has less than 50 students or upward of 5,000 young people. It has been solved. How do we know this? Because in each school, everywhere, we have at least one teacher who has cracked the DaVinci Code. We have at least one teacher who, despite the limitations of the budget, leadership, political climate, or needs of the students, has been able to have a positive,

DOI: 10.4324/9781003492535-2

significant, and potentially life-changing impact on the young people they teach. Most likely each of us has had at least one teacher who helped us become the caring professional we are. The vast majority of schools have multiple—maybe dozens, maybe more—outstanding educators, but every school has at least one. And that is where we start.

If you have children, want to have children, or have ever been a child, then you know the excitement of a student bouncing out of school and onto the bus or into the car stoked about what happened at school that day. Maybe it was the first time they learned about dinosaurs. Maybe it was the smile and warm welcome that their teacher started and ended the day with. Maybe it was the note on an essay that said, "You should become a writer!" The teacher who had the most impact might be the one who gave you extra time or assistance precisely when you needed it. Maybe it was the one who explained a new concept in a way you could best understand it. And maybe, just maybe, it was the teacher who you thought really liked you. I don't know, but you know. Your children know. And the students in your school know. They know who that one teacher was. And, let's be honest, for many students it may have been the same teacher for a number of their peers.

We all are aware of truly outstanding teachers in our schools. We are also aware of others who might not meet this standard. Just envision what our schools would be like if all the teachers were like the very best teachers. How would that impact the culture and climate in the school and in each classroom? How would that impact learning, whether it be state standards, developing a love of reading, or learning how to treat others? What would that do to lower the dropout rate? How would that impact student behavior in the classrooms and beyond? How would it impact our communities and society? How would that change the lives of all of the young people that enter our school buildings? Isn't this what you want your school to become? Isn't this what you want for your own child? Isn't this what every student deserves?

> **Just envision what our schools would be like if all the teachers were like the very best teachers.**

There are dramatic differences in the quality of teachers in every school. If all teachers could be more like the best teachers, then we would have significant improvement in every school. Every building has special teachers who connect with all students and consistently engage them in learning. This really is possible. We just have to help all teachers become like the best teachers. Let's get started. The kids are waiting.

Changing the World, One Teacher at a Time and All Teachers at Once

This book is designed to help 'society' by sharing ideas on how to increase the quality of teachers at a macro level. That means all teachers, everywhere. The book also hopes to provide specifics that can increase the effectiveness of all teachers at the micro level—in each classroom and school. Luckily, these two things are not contradictory and instead provide a synergy that we can all support. Let's start with the big picture so that everyone in the school community and the surrounding community can understand how they can assist. Ninety plus percent of this book is focused on specific things you can do in your setting. However, I would be remiss, just in case state-level decision makers read it, to not do a little framing that is outside of the direct influence of a school or district. The reason this is the balance—so school focused—is that many times sharing things at the macro level can be demoralizing because we realize we have little influence over these variables. And that is the opposite of the aim of the book. So, I want to just share a very brief synopsis of a few things that could make a big-picture difference.

One Pool of Teachers

I work with all types of schools and their educators. Public schools, private schools, and charter schools. The reason I work with all types is that they all have students in them. And I want every student to have an outstanding educational experience. You may have your own perspective about the differing types of schools and which one you value most. However, it is essential that we realize that while there may be these three types of schools—public, private, and charter—there are not three pools of teachers. There is one pool of teachers that everyone draws from. If we attack teachers in any type of school, the size and quality of the whole pool of teachers diminishes. When there are political attacks in a general way on the teachers in any of the groups, there will be fewer teachers for each of the other groups to select from. Narrowing the number of people in the teaching profession does nothing to raise the quality of the education pool.

> **There is one pool of teachers that everyone draws from. If we attack teachers in any type of school, the size and quality of the whole pool of teachers diminishes.**

In every state and country, the demonization of teachers must stop. Everything from attacks on the entire profession to nonsensical things like spreading false rumors about kitty litter in the classrooms so kids who identify as furries can use them for bathrooms. When people make up the small specific attacks like kitty litter and dishonestly spread them like truths, it wears on the caring professionals who know they are untrue. They have to then waste energy trying to defend their school to people in the grocery store, and they get disheartened by the embarrassingly unknowledgeable people on social media. It is annoying when an anonymous individual promotes these untruths, and it can be destructive to the state when people in political positions repeat them or fan the flames of school attacks. I have worked with state boards of education, state legislatures, etc. I work to help them understand that when they repeat an untruth, the people who share it do not understand it is an untruth and they repeat these falsehoods as fact. One time a group asked me how I was so confident that none of the schools in their state had kitty litter in their classrooms. I asked them if any of the students in their state had cell phones. As you can imagine, they said of course they do. I then asked if any of the students' phones had cameras. Once again, they quickly affirmed that they did. Then I asked how many pictures they have seen of kitty litter in specific schools. Weirdly none of them had ever seen one picture of kitty litter in their schools. Amazingly that is all it took for them to realize the harm that can occur when they choose to share things that attack schools.

When these negative events occur, it becomes increasingly difficult to draw teachers into the profession, and it becomes more of a challenge to keep our dedicated professionals motivated and in our schools. However, it is essential that we do so regardless of the environment that many schools and districts face. So, let's take a look at some of our options to add people to our profession and increase the likelihood of them maintaining their essential role in education. Both of these challenges are more difficult than ever, but they are also more essential.

Attract and Retain

We need to attract and retain more teachers, principals, and everyone to the education profession. The more candidates there are to choose from, the better choices we can make. Individual schools and districts can do some of these things, and all of them can have an impact on a larger state or national level. Let's take a look at a few that seem to be having a significant impact in some locations. Remember that the more educators there are, that increases the likelihood of attracting and selecting highly talented people. Here are a couple of the numerous things that can help grow the quantity so we can then focus on the quality.

Salaries: Pay is a significant motivator/demotivator in any profession, and it is definitely impacting education. One of the reasons it is currently so essential is that when there is almost no unemployment, that means there are jobs for anyone who works in a school to pursue that are outside of education. When employment opportunities are so abundant, it is even more important for salaries to be increased, and the competition from other professions is more challenging. The state/national level is the most important place to increase teacher salaries if we want to increase/ retain the number of people in the profession. If an individual district increases pay, that is great for that district and their staff, but it does not increase the appeal for current educators to remain as teachers or others to opt into the educational field. And to be honest, the ability to increase pay at the local level everywhere is fairly limited. Typically, the vast majority of a school district's budget already goes to salaries—so increasing it without additional revenue is not the jump needed to increase the likelihood of young people pursuing an educational career.

Childcare: Many schools and districts have started providing easier access to childcare for their faculty and staff. Having on-site or location-convenient childcare is a great draw to attract and retain teachers and other employees. Again, if this were funded at the state level, it could increase the numbers of educators, rather than schools just competing with each other. However, it could allow people to stay in the profession if they had easy access compared with alternative jobs.

Housing: A number of places have realized that their location is too expensive to support teachers or too isolated to have housing options. By increasing these options, we are potentially increasing the draw for candidates.

Flexible Schedules: Teachers often are restricted from being able to have flexibility to schedule doctors' appointments, etc. This could be something to offer that may be able to be done at an individual site or at a district level.

Four-Day School Week: Many states have school districts that have gone to a four-day school week. Typically, they do not have students on Mondays, and then have a longer school day than is traditional on Tuesday–Friday. Some schools have teachers work on Mondays, and others have them work one Monday a month. The idea originally started in rural areas to help control costs—less days to bus, cut down on lunch costs, utilities, etc. The unintended positive consequence was that it increased attendance, recruitment, and retention of teachers. These things need to be adopted on a statewide basis. If they only occur within a state or region of the state, and some individual districts do it and others do not, then it potentially cannibalizes teachers from our neighbors rather than growing the overall quantity of educators. If it were done on a state level, would it possibly attract more young people to the profession?

Class Sizes/Planning Time: One of the biggest challenges educators face, which makes them more likely to depart the profession, isn't the hours. Lots of professional jobs have long hours. Rather, it is the intensity of the job that makes education so wearing. Additional funding at the state level can allow for smaller class sizes to support student learning and increase the length of planning time so teachers can reduce their 'off the clock' planning, grading, etc.

There are dozens of ideas that have been suggested, and hopefully this provides some ideas or talking points for a couple of them if you have a chance to have a broad statewide impact. Now, let's move to things that I know you can implement immediately in your district, school, and setting to help all teachers become like the best teachers.

2

The Teacher Is the Variable That Matters the Most (By Far)

With a constant influx of new laws, programs, and ideas, it is easy to become overwhelmed in education. We put so much pressure on ourselves and get pinged with suggestions, demands, and policies so often that it is easy to lose sight of why we are in education and what our priorities should be. When we are constantly bombarded with input that "This is the most important thing in the world," "No wait, this is the most important thing in the world," "Oh, hold on, forget everything you were told, now this is the most important thing in the world," it is easy to become overwhelmed and lost.

The New/Old AI: Artificial Intelligence?

Wow! No wonder we are all exhausted. Is AI—Artificial Intelligence—the savior or the devil? Will it increase productivity or increase plagiarism? Will it create a robot to help with heart surgery or create a robot to take over Denver? What about school discipline? Is it a bad word now? Is assertive discipline the problem or the solution? What is our priority—the students who are

DOI: 10.4324/9781003492535-3

behaving, or those who are misbehaving? What about restorative practices? Do they always work, or do they never work?

After the pandemic, one of the things that seems to have increased in classrooms is the number of students who are behind academically, and behaviorally, and socially, and emotionally... Whew! And all of these things are true simultaneously. Yet, it seems like, even in my school with our leader and our budget and our community, somehow or another we have teachers that still seem successful. These teachers seem to get the students to behave. Their kids seem calmer, more focused, and even kinder to each other and to the teacher. How is that possible? And can all of us 'get lucky' with the students we are assigned, like the outstanding teachers seem to do every year? Is it just a roll of the dice, or is it possible that this teacher is doing some things that we could all be doing, which would allow us to be as fortunate?

What is even more confusing is that some of these exceptional teachers will immediately embrace AI and others will be much more hesitant—or maybe even resistant—to do so. Yet whichever choice they make, it seems to work. How can this be? And, more importantly, can it be true for me? Then it hits you. All the best teachers in your school use AI and they use it every day. Only with them, AI stands for Actual Intelligence. And apparently that never goes out of favor. So, how do we replicate that!? Let's see if we can make sense out of seemingly no sense.

Pandemic: Virtual Teaching

Teaching during the pandemic was incredibly challenging. Many schools went virtual, seemingly overnight. One thing that made it so difficult is we didn't get to have a dress rehearsal; we just went to opening night. If we could have practiced for a week or even a few days with students when we were all still in the classroom together, the transition would have been smoother. Not perfect, but clearly better than how we had to do it with little or no preparation. Yet, even though in most schools we all did this simultaneously, with no practice, somehow, we knew certain teachers would have more success than others. Of course, knowledge of and comfort with technology were important, but there was something else, wasn't there? If it was not just technical skill with technology, what was it?

With no preparation and everyone in a school going virtual at the same time, could you name a few teachers you felt were more likely to figure it out and have more success than most others? Contrastingly, could you name some teachers you thought would have a more challenging, or almost impossible, time figuring out successful virtual teaching? And when we returned to more traditional, in-person teaching, did you realize that the teachers you thought were going to be the most challenged with distance instruction often seemed to be the most challenged when students returned to their classrooms? Why is this?

The real reason is that it is the same skill set. What makes a teacher successful virtually has a very strong connection to what makes them successful in person. And conversely, the opposite also applies. Because we know it is the person rather than the technology. Always has been, always will be. We bring in new programs and the same teachers thrive. Our school adopts a new classroom management approach, and the same teachers have the most success with the new program that had it with the previous program. And, way too often, the ones that struggled before continue to struggle, even though the structure is different. Let's take a look at another example.

Flexible Seating

Flexible seating is a very popular trend in education. The basic concept is to move away from traditional rows of seats and design the classroom to increase engagement by allowing students to choose the type of seating that best fits their learning style. Often there is a combination of tables, bean bags, differing types of chairs and desk, couches, etc., that students can select from.

Some people feel flexible seating is the solution to increasing student learning and improves student behavior by allowing choice. Others feel that it inhibits student learning because of a lack of structure and that it may increase student misbehavior. Why do these types of debates exist so often in education? It's because both sides are right and both sides are wrong. It's basically a deadlock for a couple of reasons. The first is that everyone who is debating it has picked a small sample and assumed it can be generalized. Often commentators have an N of 1 in their 'research.' But the most likely reason we cannot come to an agreement is that the debaters have not identified the correct variable.

Here is something I do with groups when presenting. I ask them this series of four questions:

> **How many of you can name at least one outstanding teacher that would be outstanding using flexible seating?** Almost every hand in the audience goes up.
> **How many of you can name at least one outstanding teacher that would be outstanding *not* using flexible seating?** Almost every hand in the audience goes up.
> **How many of you can name at least one struggling teacher that would struggle using flexible seating?** Again, almost every hand goes up.
> **How many of you can name at least one struggling teacher that would struggle *not* using flexible seating?** Once again, almost every hand goes up.

So, what is *not* the variable in these four questions? Flexible seating. What is most often the variable with any program or idea that is implemented in a school? The teacher.

What is most often the variable with any program or idea that is implemented in a school? The teacher.

Students with Trauma

Schools have always dealt with students who have had to deal with things we hope they never have to deal with. Abuse, neglect, disasters, violence, and other things that can cause lasting emotional distress. Over the last few years, these numbers have seemingly been increasing, and for sure educators have become more aware and sensitive to them. I am a huge mental health proponent. I am a true believer in the importance of needing support to deal with significant things that impact students and adults. However, what sometimes happens is we begin to use a word like trauma to describe any level of issue. What happens when there becomes a new or more recognizable term is that sometimes it becomes the label for all situations. Any student who struggles academically must have suffered trauma, or if a student misbehaves on any level, it must be trauma. This is not at all diminishing the significance of it. Sometimes it seems like every student has trauma. But it is amazing how many students, when they are in the very best teachers' classrooms, behave very differently. They are able to cope with their issues in a way that they are not able to in other settings. This does not mean they are not victims of trauma. Some students are so impacted by life events they do not have as much success as we would hope, even in the best settings. However, if the very best teacher can create an environment that makes students feel safer, more secure, and more cared for, then we get to see the impact that a different setting can have on many students.

Too many of us have seen or been in classrooms or work environments where there is a great deal of dysfunction. When there is not an effective leader/teacher, we may all feel like we are dealing with trauma every day, and none of us respond as appropriately to the situation as we wish we could.

Great teachers do not have the ability to 'fix' students who have had debilitating events happen in their life. However, when many students that we thought were impossible to deal with are in the classrooms of the best teachers, we realize that if we can create this environment throughout our school, then we have a chance of providing the care and support this student and all students deserve. These teachers show us what is possible. It is our responsibility to provide this for every child in our school. And simultaneously we must provide extra professional help for the students who have been seriously affected by life events.

Participation Trophies

I was nervous to write this section, as I know this is a big deal to many people. On a regular basis I hear people on podcasts, talk shows, or in stores talking about what a problem participation trophies are and how they have impacted the younger generations. Others say that it is the bane of the Western world—it's everything that is wrong with society today. Wow, that is quite a powerful statement. Basically, 'participation trophies' is a term used to describe an event where everyone receives recognition for being a part of the team. One of the most common times we see it is when three- and four-year-olds, at the end of a T-ball season, all receive a trophy or certification acknowledging they played on a team.

Ironically, I work with athletic team coaches at a variety of levels—little league, high school, collegiate. And primarily in basketball. Anyhow, coaches ask me to come and watch their practices and offer guidance on ways they can be more impactful. My advice isn't technical—it's not the best offense to run or how to play a zone defense. It's really about how to get the players to do what it is you want/need them to do. How to be more cooperative, try harder, have more confidence, etc.

One time a high-level coach asked me to attend practice and give him feedback. I went to his practice and asked him what the problem was. He shared that he cannot motivate the players because "they have all received participation trophies."

I was a little taken aback and said, "These trophies must be pretty powerful." He said they were ruining everything "because the players don't have to earn anything. When we were little, we had to earn everything!" I asked him, "Do you know who else received participation trophies?" He half yelled, "No, who?!"

I said the team that beat you last night. They all received participation trophies as well—every player, I'd assume. And the team that beat you a week ago. And I'd guess, the team that you play Friday. My bet is all of them have received participation trophies as well.

One thing that affects all of us is that sometimes we look for excuses and sometimes we look for solutions. The people who are more impactful and effective look for solutions, but there are others who consistently center their focus on excuses. And, sadly, many people who center on the blame-frame like to associate with others who do the same.

People who hunt for and find excuses actually hope the excuses are the problem. It is so much more comforting for a coach/teacher/parent/supervisor to blame participation trophies than it is to look in the mirror. The best leaders and teachers do not center on participation trophies. The least effective ones find great comfort in pointing fingers.

How many of you can think of a child you know or a student you have who might have been a little better off if they had ever received a participation trophy? Go into the best, more well-rounded student's bedroom. What is it full of? Participation trophies, but you already knew that, didn't you? Do you have at least one student, at least one, who is struggling academically, socially, emotionally, and behaviorally? Is the biggest challenge that student faces that they have received too many participation trophies in their life? Is it that they have been loved too much? That they have been cared for too much? Of course not. We all know, if we set aside our biases, that it is exactly the opposite for the children who struggle so much.

Children know by the time they are five or six that participation trophies do not mean anything. Maybe it would be beneficial if the adults realized that as well.

The best teachers do not focus on things they cannot control.

The best teachers do not focus on things they cannot control. Instead, one of the things that makes them so successful, so special, is that they are laser centered on things they can influence. Let's look at how the best teachers look at the world and see how we can help others use the same lenses when they see their own students. We really all can look at the world like the best people do. We just have to first figure out what the best people do. And I'll give you a hint. You can do it as well!

3

How Great Teachers Look at the World

Hint—You Can Do It Too

A Goal and a Wish

Recently I presented to a group of about a thousand principals. And like I typically do, if I have a chance before the session starts, I like to mingle with the group. Meet people, glad hand, make connections. Building relationships and being friendly is part of my purpose. But one other goal is to try to find the most talented people in the room. The reason is very simple. The most talented people are the ones I can learn the most from. You can learn from anyone, but you can really raise your game by connecting with the most successful and gifted people. So often they do things you have never thought of. And if you have thought of something, you really feel special if other highly successful people are doing it as well. It is very reinforcing.

Anyhow, this particular day my session was on *Leading School Change* (2010), which is one of my books. I found a group of outstanding principals and one in particular was a shining

DOI: 10.4324/9781003492535-4

light. Because the title of the conference was Leading School Change, I asked her what goal she has regarding something she would like to change in her school. She said, "I'd like each student, when they leave home, to be excited about learning!" We both smiled and I paused and said, "That is not a goal, it's a wish." She asked why it's a wish. I said a goal is something you can influence. A wish is something you need magic pixie dust to influence. She didn't understand. I asked if she was married, and she said yes. I then smilingly shared, "If you'd like to start exercising, that is a goal. If you'd like your spouse to start exercising, that is a wish." She laughed, and I had one more example.

I asked her, "How do students walk into your best teacher's classroom?" Her eyes lit up and she said, "They are excited about learning!" I then asked her, "How did they leave home?" She hesitated and then said, "I don't have any idea."

Then I asked, "How do students walk into an ineffective teacher's classroom?" She sadly replied, "They are not very excited about learning." I then asked her, "How did they leave home?" She quietly repeated, "I don't have any idea."

> **The best teachers consistently focus on what they can influence. Other, less effective people focus on what they can't influence.**

A goal is how they enter a teacher's classroom; a wish is how they leave home. The best teachers consistently focus on what they can influence. Other, less effective people focus on what they can't influence.

The First Day of Teaching During the Pandemic

I promise this book will not entirely be about the pandemic of 2020, but I'd like to reflect one more time on how the view of the best teachers can vary versus that of most other teachers. We have already reflected on being able to identify staff members who were more likely than others to be successful in suddenly having to alter their teaching approach. But let's take a minute to delve into what specifically makes certain educators excel. As we found, one of the biggest challenges of teaching during the pandemic was that there was little or no preparation. So how do the most successful people look at things?

Picture the first day of teaching (and some of you were students then—so think of it from the student view as well) and the first time teaching during the pandemic. There are supposed to be live students to work with, and a teacher opens up their computer to connect with their class. They have 25 students on their roster, and 11 show up the first day, which may be a kind estimate. Anyhow, what is the first goal of the great teacher? You might guess it is to reconnect with students, make them feel welcome, assure them they are safe, rebuild relationships, etc. And no question, each of these are different approaches that effective teachers take. But an underlying purpose is to make sure the number of students attending never goes down to 10. The very first instinct of outstanding people is to be successful influencing the people and things they can influence. They know nothing about the other 14 who are not in attendance, but they know they have the opportunity, right there and then, to connect with and hopefully retain the 11 that are there. And, of course, if they do a good enough job that first day, they potentially have 11 young salespeople who might be able to assist with the 14 peers who are unaccounted for.

Outstanding teachers have varying paths to follow, but they all have the same destination. Whether the first approach was to check on well-being, reestablish relationships, or just help students feel less alone, the aim was to make sure the students became connected and engaged so that they returned the next day. By focusing on those we can impact, we maximize those we will impact. Eleven students joined the class so I am going to treat them with such respect and dignity that for sure they will be back. And, maybe with a plus one.

What about other staff members who may not have the same results? They, just like most of the other teachers, only had a fraction of their students show up. Let's say it was the exact same, 11 out of 25. Their immediate focus—and potentially it's still their focus years later—was the 14 that didn't show up. Instantly they centered on, "What could I do, 14 kids weren't even there! And after a week I was down to 6! You can't blame me for that!"

The locus of control is something they quickly saw as out of their influence. This has the effect of avoiding blame. It also has the impact of avoiding growth. And the more people who view the world like this connect with others with the same helpless external focus, the more reinforced they feel. It really is a 'It's Not My Fault' mentality.

This does not mean that outstanding teachers never extend their perspective outside of the 11 students who were in attendance the first day. Not at all. It's just that their first instincts are to make those who are there feel welcomed and valued and then expand their circle. Impact what you can *and then see* if you can impact more. It's funny because we often hear, "Don't just get the low-hanging fruit." And this is true. However, it is probably even sillier to leave the easiest fruit to access hanging on the tree. Have success gathering the low-hanging fruit, and it may give you the energy to go after harder-to-reach targets.

The Learning Relationship: The Core of the High-Quality Teacher

One other thing that is always at the core of a high-quality teacher is that they produce high-quality teaching. As we just discussed, the first day of the pandemic many teachers checked on student well-being. Others made sure they were safe. A great number were attempting to reestablish relationships from when they met in person prior to the pandemic. Another group of teachers had a different approach. They just started teaching. Yep, they just started teaching. Some of us may recoil when we read that sentence. They just started teaching?! Didn't they build relationships? Didn't they check on how the kids were doing? How offensive. Aren't we supposed to be about relationships, relationships, relationships? At least that seems to be the drumbeat the last few years. Build a relationship before you can get the students to care about learning? These statements are not totally untrue, but remember, the highly effective teachers have similar goals, but they travel differing paths to reach them.

Let's think for a minute about that statement. Some teachers just started teaching when the students returned. At first blush that may seem ridiculous or even offensive. But I'd like you to think of this. The likelihood of that approach working is probably connected to how good the teacher is at teaching. Some readers may recoil when you read this. Wait, that is not Maslow before Bloom—the famous phrase that suggests that for students to learn, their basic needs (physiological, safety, belonging) must be met first. Of course, if a student is at an extreme point in their survival needs, it would prevent all learning—and probably their ability to join a Zoom—but the point is not ignoring or making light of that. Not in the least. Instead, the point is that some teachers are very gifted at teaching, and embedded in their approach is the reassurance that they care about you as a person. Embedded in their approach is the fact that when they make you feel capable of learning, it helps you feel safer, and they clearly make you feel loved and that you belong.

When you were younger (years ago, or last week—you get to choose) did you ever read a book that made you feel safe, special, significant? Have you ever watched a movie, TV show, TikTok, or commercial that gave you a boost? Did you ever become so engaged that you forgot you missed lunch or even lost track of time? Maybe, just maybe, you may have had a teacher—maybe just one—who made you feel this way as well. The connectivity is not sacrificed by teaching effectively. Instead, it is intertwined. They reinforce each other. In a great teacher's class, the students feel safe, they feel confident, and they feel significant. It is not relationships versus teaching. It is combined in a **learning relationship**. The great teachers are able to effectively teach and build relationships simultaneously. They do not need a week of isolated 'getting to know you' activities. They have a year to have that journey with their students.

> **The great teachers are able to effectively teach and build relationships simultaneously.**

Some great teachers start the school year by having scavenger hunts or 'getting to know you' activities, some start by sharing the rules, procedures, and expectations of the class, and some start by just teaching highly effectively. However, within a short period of time, all the great teachers start teaching highly effectively. That is how we know they are exceptional, and that is what makes them special. It isn't Maslow's Hierarchy before Bloom's Taxonomy. The same way great teachers do not need to rank, sort, or select their favorites, they move up everyone as needed together.

We often hear that students do not remember what we taught them; instead, they remember how we treated them. This is true for some less effective teachers. However, in the great teachers' class-rooms, students remember both. Can you recall a book or story that your favorite teacher read to the class? Do you recall an important time in history and its impact on society today? What is 5 times 7? Do you remember to have your hands on the steering wheel in the 10 and 2 position? I know some of you just said, "No, it is now 9 and 3!" Hmm, I guess that proves the point.

The more they cared about you, the more you cared about the content. We listen to people that listen to us. We care about what they say when they care about what we say. If this gets accom-plished through start of the year activities, by all means keep using them. But without achieving a learning relationship, these approaches will not have the impact we desire. A school year is a long time (I don't have to tell you that). The foundation of that is learning, and the best way to learn is to have a connection. Put these two together and we have the Learning Relationship that we all desire. We will expand on this later in the book, but I wanted to include it as a foundational point now.

What's Next?

Now that we have a sense of how great teachers look at the world and some of the ways they are different from their peers, what can be done to help every teacher become an outstanding teacher? How can we help everyone become the teacher we remember having as a student, the teacher that we long to become so that we can have a lasting impact on our students? Is it possible to be that 'it' teacher we aimed to become when we first started the pathway to teaching? And is it possible to have a school, district, and state that has an increasing number of outstanding teachers so that we can give the students what they deserve? The answer is yes. So, let's see how.

Part II

Hiring Exceptional Teachers

4

Two Core Ways to Increase Teacher Quality in Your Setting
Let's Start with Hiring Highly Talented Teachers

There are really two main ways to improve the quality of teaching (and every other profession). One is to hire and develop better teachers. The other is to improve the teachers that we have. It cannot be one or the other. It must be both. In Chapter 1, I briefly described a few general ideas for increasing the number of teachers entering the profession and reducing the outflow of teachers departing the profession. The reason I did not spend more time on this is that the majority of readers of this book and people in education do not have a position that can influence increasing salaries across the nation or even at the state level. And, since outstanding people focus on what they can influence instead of what they cannot, this book is attempting to follow a similar pattern. Though we may think that superintendents can boost salaries, once we understand budgeting, we realize that it is much more of a tweak than anything else. Remember if a superintendent does not increase salaries, they do not keep the remaining monies for themselves.

DOI: 10.4324/9781003492535-6

And since such a high percentage of district budgets is salaries, the flexibility is minimal. So, let's take a look at places we can make a difference: hiring and developing outstanding teachers.

Any teacher can improve, the same as any principal, superintendent, custodian, etc. However, we also are aware that there is a wide variance in the talents of candidates and applicants. If you think of talent on a 1–10 scale, most people have a range of natural talent. Then the goal of a leader is maximizing where they can fall in this range. For example, one candidate has a range of being a 4 through a 7. In other words, with less effective leadership, they will be a 4, and with highly effective leadership they will be a 7. Others may be a 2 to a 6, or a 6.5 to a 10. The ranges are also not the same. Someone might be a 2 to a 9 in which they have a great potential if it is maximized, but a lower floor if they are not nurtured effectively.

None of this is a criticism, and it is not shared in a mean-spirited way at all. However, if we don't think there is great variance in talent, there is really no reason to interview. We might as well select candidates from a blind draw lottery. The better we are at hiring, the better our chances of having more outstanding teachers.

What Is Talent?

One of my books is titled *What Great Teachers Do Differently* (Routledge, 2020). Sometimes people like to ask, "How do you define a great teacher?" I usually answer, "The same way you do. I don't know how to define it, but we both know what it is." It's a combination of intelligence, care, creativity, hard work, enthusiasm, energy, the ability to connect with everyone, etc. We all know. We have known, as a student and as a colleague, people who have all these qualities. People often share things like, "I know a teacher who is great with college-bound students, but not good with students who struggle with reading." Yes, we all do. They are highly skilled with certain students, but not with others. They did not quite make the great cut. That doesn't mean they can't grow in the area. It also doesn't mean that a leader shouldn't try to maximize their time with teachers they have the highest level of success with. It does mean they haven't made it to the 9/10 level. The more we emphasize their strengths and limit their weaknesses, the closer they are to maximizing their talent potential. Remember if everyone is a 10, no one is a 10. Instead, we are all automatically 5's. That does not mean we do not treat everyone like they are a 10. That doesn't mean we give up on people who have a ceiling of a 7. It just means we are aware that everyone is not the same. Talent is defined for our purposes as the total package. It is intelligence, and work ethic, and ability to connect with all students, and ...

Now, let's see how we can add some highly talented staff members to our schools and districts by looking at the hiring practice in a different way than traditionally done. No reason to do what we have done previously unless we have only been adding, 8's, 9's, and mostly 10's. If that isn't what we have been adding, there's no reason to not look for a different way.

All We Want Is Talent

Now, please remember, talent is not one dimensional. It is not just intelligence. It is not just experience. It is not just people who are positive. It is finding someone who is all these things. When you add the right person, it changes much more than one classroom. When we hire correctly, we change a grade level, team, and/or department. I work with many school districts and if they are struggling, many times it is because they do not have one truly outstanding principal who can help guide/point/lead the way for other building leaders. If you do not have any one person who is great, it is very difficult to elevate everyone to that level. If you get one great talent, you can add others and also maximize the talent in those who are current employees. It is much easier to steal ideas from others than think of them yourself. Also, the true talents eliminate the excuses from people who use them as a crutch. One outstanding person shows that it is possible in your setting, with your students, and your budget, and your community. Struggling people sometimes hope it isn't possible and may at times even root against breakthrough individuals. Well, let's worry about that

Work at hiring. It is so much more fun to put effort into hiring than it is to put effort into remediating.

once we get some more break-through individuals! Work at hiring. It is so much more fun to put effort into hiring than it is to put effort into remediating.

Checking References

Checking references is such a common practice. The majority of places do this. What is scary is that it is the majority, not the entirety. Let's think about what it takes to check references. Does it take intelligence? Nope. Does it take knowledge? Again, no. Does it take effort? This one is a yes. So, why do we often not do an effective job in checking references? One reason is that so often we are hiring during the time of year that we are most exhausted. We are hiring for the next year as we are finishing up and quite drained from the intense part of the previous school year. Thus, we may not do as good of a job as we could. Do you know one reason we are so drained? It's because the average and below-average people in our schools have worn us down! Are you exhausted because of the number of students your three best teachers send to the office with discipline referrals? Of course not. Have the parent complaints just poured in regarding your top five staff members? Obviously not. Instead, when you get down or even feel kind of defeated, just slip into your best teachers' classrooms. Then you remember what school is. You are amazed at the game they bring every day. You are so proud to be their leader. And so proud to be the leader of their school. If all the teachers were like these teachers, would that change your energy level at every point of the year, including the last? So, let's look at checking references.

Many candidates list three or so references, and most people contact some or all of them. Of course, we chose our references to list on our resume for a reason. My main one is trying to find three people who will lie for me or at least round up. Kidding, I hope. Anyhow, most people choose those who will represent them in the best light. Clearly, we should call all three. However, to me, hiring is the most important thing I can do to improve my school, so I go beyond that. Remember, our goal is great. We want to find that talent! Average people are more comfortable with average people. That is why you can so often find exceptional people. Average people don't want them around. Some people don't want them in their school because it makes them feel inadequate. Leaders may not want them because you know they know. Average leaders know that the best employees know they are average, so they'd actually prefer if they weren't there. And the last thing they want to do is add more outstanding people! That is why you have a chance to get them as long as you have the urge to want them to be part of your setting. So, let's put in work now, so we don't have to put in the remedial work later if we can avoid it.

If I get an applicant that has been in seven schools and lists three references, I call every school—why would you not? If I receive a resume that mentions a school where they student-taught nine years ago, I call that school. Why wouldn't you? If you find someone gifted, many others might recognize that gift also. However, let's tweak the questions we ask when we contact references.

Would You Hire Them Again?

Would you like to take a guess as to what the most common question people in any profession ask whenever they check references? Since this section is titled, "Would you hire them again?" I am hoping that is your guess. And you'd be correct. However, remember we want outstanding people. Not run-of-the-mill employees. So, what percent of the time would you guess the answer to the "Would you hire them again?" question is yes? Maybe 80 to 90 percent? Maybe more? There is a chance that even if the person just posted something embarrassing on social media, they may have made that cut. That standard is so low, it is almost ridiculous. However, there's nothing wrong with asking a softball question to make someone feel comfortable. So, keep that as your number one question if you'd like. But I'd like to share a couple of additions.

After you ask, "Would you hire them again?" and likely receive an affirmative response, then ask this question:

"Would you recruit them?" Is that a completely different question than would you hire them again? Yep. Whether they say yes or no, then ask this:

"How many teachers do you have in your school?" Let's say they say 50. (The number doesn't matter. It's just an example.) Then ask this:

"How many of your 50 teachers would you recruit?" The reason to ask this question is so you potentially know how discriminating the person you are asking is. If they say they'd recruit 10, is that quite different than if they say they'd recruit 45? If you do not know how picky someone is, you gain little knowledge by asking for a candidate's strengths and weaknesses. No matter what their answer is, but let's say it is 10, ask this:

"Where does this candidate fall in the 10? Are they the first teacher you'd recruit, the fifth teacher you'd recruit, or the tenth teacher you'd recruit?" Does that help you know more than a typical general question? Now, let's say they say seventh. But their answer is irrelevant to your next question which you are already prepared to ask. After they say 7, ask this:

"Why aren't they first? What keeps them from being first? What is the difference between them and the first?" Does that help you understand the quality of your candidate in the eyes of the reference you have contacted? But what about specific areas that you'd like to learn more about?

The 1 to 10 Scale

The question process we just shared helps you get a general sense of where the skill/talent level of the candidate may be. However, what if there are specific things you want to know such as leadership skills, work ethic, innovation level, classroom management, etc.? Well, here is an example of the format you can use with questions that might assist with that. We will choose classroom management, but you will of course select what matters most to you.

Here is an example of a new question chain involving classroom management (or whatever matters most to you). Ask:

"On a 1 to 10 scale, how are they on classroom management?" Typically, people say "8, 9, or 10." Let's say they say a 9. Now, you already have the context of the selectivity of the reference you are communicating with, which is helpful, but then ask this:

"Of your 50 teachers, how many 10's do you have in classroom management?" Your view of your candidate might be quite different if the person says 6 or 46. But no matter what they say you can ask this:

"Why aren't they a 10? What keeps them from being a 10? What is the difference between them and a 10?" The example was about classroom management, but remember, you can do this with any specific area you want to focus on.

But if the person responded to your previous question of, "On a 1 to 10 scale, how are they on classroom management" by saying 10, then ask these three questions:

"How many 10's do you have out of 50?" If they say any number, but let's say 15, then ask this:

"Where do they rank in your 10's?" Are they first, seventh, or fifteenth?" Let's say they say seventh, then ask this:

"Why aren't they first? What is keeping them from being first? What is the difference between them and the first?"

The more specific your questions are, the more precise and informative the answers are likely to be as well. The goal is not to trick anyone; the goal is to learn. Take your time, ask kindly, and make them feel comfortable. Most of us have never been asked questions like this before, which makes it more likely that they will be truthful. To answer these questions requires a much higher level of precise thinking than typical, generalized questions. Feel free to alter the questions to get the information and focus you need.

But hopefully the structure provided a different way of thinking as you work toward your new goal of hiring excellence.

What you are really doing by asking these questions is forcing the person you contacted regarding the reference to think how the best leaders already think. Say you asked an exceptional principal, "How many employees could you not live without?"

Typically, they reply surprisingly quickly. Do you know why they are so speedy? It's because they think about it all the time. They continually think, "Who can I not live without? Who are the keys to moving the school forward? What can I do to support these key talents?" Other leaders often do not see people in such a way. They often reply generally in ways like, "Everyone is good" or "We have a lot of good educators here." There is nothing wrong in replying that way, as long as that is not the way the leader thinks themselves. If we do not understand and appreciate our best people, believe me, someone else will.

If we do not understand and appreciate our best people, believe me, someone else will.

5

The Number One Goal in Hiring

If you have heard me speak or read some of my books, this is old news. However, there is a difference between saying it, knowing it, and living it. It is essential that we remember *the number one goal anytime we hire someone is to have our school become more like the new teacher, not to have the new teacher become like the school.* We may not always achieve that aim, but the best leaders always reach for that target.

There are several things we can share during the recruitment process that are very attractive to talented people. Here is a message I always shared to attract the best. It was the truth, so it was easy to share with conviction:

We do not hire new teachers to fall in line; we hire new teachers to form new lines. We don't try to hire what we have; we try to hire what we **We do not hire new teachers to fall in line; we hire new teachers to form new lines.** don't have. There is no pecking order in our school. There is no seniority list. If you have an opinion, we want you to share your opinion. If we didn't want your opinion, we wouldn't hire you. If we hire you, it's because we want your opinion. If you want to make a difference from day one, this is the place to be. If you don't want to make a difference, we understand that a lot of

DOI: 10.4324/9781003492535-7

people don't want to work that hard, and there are many other schools that would welcome you.

Which candidates would you guess are most drawn to this? The most talented! Do you know why this rings true—especially in education? The best people want to make a difference. And they want to make a difference now. That is why they chose education. And they have spent their whole life—no matter whether they are 22 or 62—looking for a place where they can have this kind of an impact. Everyone has been in settings—classrooms as students, part-time or previous jobs, friend groups—where the complainers receive the vast majority of the attention. Way too often people work to cater to those who are the best at whining. And you know what, the best people cannot stand it.

Instead, do you know what highly talented people are looking for? They want to find a place where they fit. A place that has people who think like them. It doesn't matter how old they are, what gender they are, or what their background is, they want to find a place that values their talents and gifts. And you want to know something else? You can be that place because most leaders and locations are uncomfortable with difference makers. It is scary for many, whether they are colleagues or the 'boss.' The same way they want to be the breakthrough teacher, understand they are going to help you lead the breakthrough school. Do not settle. Every time you settle, you miss a chance at great. This is a costly opportunity lost. Hire the difference makers. Bring them in, let them run, and make them feel special. We will talk more about how to have your best people assist in moving the school forward, but first we need as many 'best people' as possible.

An increasingly common approach in hiring in education is having team interviews for prospective candidates. The team may include teachers, parents, administrators, and even students. There is nothing right or wrong about the team approach. However, it is like flexible seating in that the determination of its effectiveness is the person/people, not the concept. This same thing applies to group interviews.

The purpose of an interview is to find and hire the very best candidate. And the goal is for that candidate to be truly outstanding—highly talented. If putting a team together will increase the likelihood of sorting out candidates to find the best, and the team approach will result in the best candidate being attracted to the school, then it is a true no brainer. However, is there any chance that some team members might not want people who are a threat to the pecking order? Is there a chance that if there is an average teacher on the committee, they would rather not have a 9 added to their grade level? A chance that they would be more comfortable with a 6? And, if the new person is chosen against the will of someone on the team, is there any possibility that they may even work against their success?

The answer to these questions might be yes, no, or who knows. However, if we do not ask ourselves these questions in advance, we may discover an answer we do not want when it is too late. Remember that outstanding people want to work with others who have the same standards. Usually, average people want to work with others who share the same standards as they do, as do low achievers. The committee approach, like so many other programs and ideas in education, is neither right nor wrong. Whether the approaches are done correctly is the determinant of whether they are right or wrong.

Remember that outstanding people want to work with others who have the same standards.

One of the most common uses of a team approach is when a school is hiring a new assistant principal. This seems logical. And one of the reasons this is done is to help the selected candidate become more accepted when they are chosen and start to work. It is seen as a way to give them instant credibility. This is a great idea... on paper. But you know the best idea? Whatever process is most likely to lead to the best candidate. That is the solution to hiring.

If you hired a new assistant principal in June and everyone is excited all summer, that is wonderful. However, if the newly chosen assistant does not handle student behavior, office referrals, and supervision effectively, no one says, "Well at least they interviewed well." No teacher who was on the committee says, "You can blame me. I chose them." Instead, it is much more likely someone says, "That wasn't who I wanted, but I felt pressure to go along with the others."

I have worked in a principal preparation program for years. Many of the students I work with have just taken their first jobs, and they are naturally nervous. They share that the school which chose them wanted an insider, and they are from outside the district, or the team wanted someone with more experience, and they are new, etc. I always share with the candidate that all of that matters until the first student is sent to the office. If you make the teachers feel supported, they do not care what your background is. If the teachers do not feel supported, they do not care what your background is. Hire for talent, and whatever process leads to that is the process that is best. Don't place short-term wins over long-term success.

Hire for talent, and whatever process leads to that is the process that is best. Don't place short-term wins over long-term success.

Interview Questions to Find the Best

It is important to always remember that the main purpose of an interview is to differentiate candidates, not make them seem the same. There are many ways to do this, including having them practice teaching, etc. However, rather than give a laundry list of ideas, I'd like to share a line of questioning that may help frame the approach you'd like to develop and implement in your setting.

Common questions in interviews are generalized things like, "Tell me your philosophy of education." This seems like a great question, at least it seems like a commonly asked question, but does it truly differentiate candidates? Does anyone ever answer, "I warn them once and then slam them against the wall?" Of course not. And though we assume no one will ever actually do this, many of us have seen staff members who emotionally approach students like this when they reach boiling point. Questions like this are so general that they allow anyone to answer. If you are a poorly prepared student but are fairly intelligent, you typically want an essay test rather than multiple choice. Because then they don't know what you don't know. Instead, you are able to shield your lack of knowledge by covering it up with the knowledge you do have, even if it is only peripherally related.

Also, another area that seems unusual, but sadly is not, is giving candidates questions like, "If you were a cookie, what kind of a cookie would you be?" People somehow think that determines if a person can 'think on their feet' or think 'outside the box.' You could argue both sides of that, I guess. My biggest fear is what the best candidate thinks when someone asks them that type of question. Plus, what is even a correct answer? You might as well ask "Should Pluto be reinstituted as a planet?" or "What's your favorite Dakota?" Do any of these help you get a sense of talent?

One way to think of questions: If you asked your current staff members your interview questions, would you know which ones to hire as a result of their answers? If not, then they are probably not the best questions and will not lead to future success. Instead, one type of question that seems to differentiate candidates is a 'true-life situational question.' This means the type of question the teacher will face in the classroom on a regular basis.

Here is one of my favorites:

"Let's say it is the first week of school and you are teaching, and a student starts talking. What would you do?" No matter how they answer, here is your next question:

"Let's say a few minutes later you are still teaching, and the student starts talking again, what would you do?" No matter how they answer, here is your next question:

"Let's say it's a few minutes later and you are still teaching, and the student starts talking once again, what would you do?"

You could keep walking down that path as many times as you want. However, ask yourself this—would all the teachers in your school answer this question the same? If the answer is no, you have differentiating questions. The purpose is not to trick anyone. Exactly the opposite. The purpose is to find out about their self-control: Do they escalate or deescalate, and so on? What percent of teachers in your school, by the second or third time, would stop teaching and behave in a way that actually escalates the situation? Can you picture people saying things to the student like, "Would you like to teach?" "Do you have something you'd like to share that is more important than what I am saying?" Do you have people who would escalate by saying they would stop teaching and stare at the student? Do you have people who by the third time would threaten to send the student to the safe room, the hallway, or even the office?

Conversely, do you have people who would say their first instinct is to keep teaching and use proximity to naturally move closer to the student? They might share that they would try to fleetingly catch the eye of the student to see if that was beneficial.

Be honest, do you have people in your current setting who would do the escalating approach and others who would take a more even approach and try to minimize the disruption? Do you wish whoever hired the former group had asked these questions in the interview so they would know to keep looking before selecting a candidate? These are called true-life situational questions. You know why you ask this type; it is because they are true-life situations that come into play starting on day one. If the tone and instincts are problematic during the interview, just wait until there are 25 students and the teacher is tired.

Do not ask ridiculous situations. I am not nearly as worried about what happens in a one-off hypothetical as I am about a likely first-day scenario. What a teacher does when a student first starts talking will apply in every classroom. What a teacher does if a kid pulls out a bong from their backpack and tries to light it in class may never occur. And if the teacher handles the first disruptions correctly, it greatly diminishes the likelihood of the larger challenges.

Tone and Manner

One other thing that will come into play every day with new (and all) staff members is tone and manner—their regular disposition. A way to hear and feel this is by continuing the question chain given earlier. After the third time you ask, "Let's say it's a few minutes later and you are still teaching and the student starts talking once again, what would you do?", then ask:

"Would you even involve the parents (guardian/family/adult)?"

Of course, every teacher, in an interview, will say yes. **In an interview**, they will always say yes. So, then ask:

"Would you ever call the parents (guardian/family/adult)?"

Of course, every teacher, in an interview, will always say yes. **In an interview**, they will always say yes. So, then say:

"Okay, I'm their parent, call me." And have them role play calling you. Don't have them describe what they would say; have them act it out. And you respond to them to carry the call forward.

Now, you may not get a perfect response—especially with newbies and during the nervousness of an interview, but what you will get is their natural tone and manner. You will get a sense of the professionalism, kindness, and care with which they communicate to others. Think about the way your best people always communicate and compare it to how others may come up short in this essential area. It is so important to know this before they are employed rather than after.

A friend of mine owns many retail businesses, and he regularly reminds me that his philosophy is to always hire for personality. One of his most repeated quotes is, "I can teach cash register, but I can't teach nice." Greatness and nice may not be 100 percent correlated, but I guarantee they have a great deal of overlap. At least in education. And hopefully in your school.

6

The Construction of Induction

Induction is a very commonly used word now, and its pithy best friend is the term onboarding. Induction is typically thought of as the process of introducing a new employee to the organization—usually for the first few days. Onboarding is a term that describes the process of socializing a new employee into the organization, and it is usually seen as taking a period of weeks or months. Often it applies to learning their job, the rules of their workplace, etc. These are both very traditional areas, even though they are presented as groundbreaking. They are not a negative; they are just not enough if our goal is to help our employees become exceptional. Remember, our goal is for our school to become more like the new teachers, rather than the reverse. The traditional implication is, how do we help newcomers 'fit in' or 'adapt' to our culture and school? This could be your goal if what you have is what you want. If everyone is highly successful and the needs of every student are met or even exceeded, then this probably should be the goal. However, regardless of the quality of your school, we are in the improvement business, not the perfection business, and I'd guess we all see areas where our setting can grow in a positive direction.

Though many districts have central office-led induction, which can be of great benefit, building-level induction is essential.

DOI: 10.4324/9781003492535-8

Someone at the district level can explain the teacher evaluation process, but we really want to learn about the evaluation process from the person who will actually be doing the evaluation. We may meet someone from central office during the initial onboarding process that we respect or even feel an admirable connection with. This is wonderful. But when school starts and we are in the heart of the action, it is much more likely that we will need to rely on those who are in our individual school.

All organizations have a culture. Ironically, people that have been in the setting for a while have the least ability to recognize what the culture is because they are used to it. If you have been in a school where everyone is friendly, you may think that is how all schools are. If you have been in a school where every teacher goes into their classroom and treats it as a silo, you might think that is what schools are like in general. It is very similar to however you grew up. If your family had large Sunday dinners, it is normal. If they eat in front of the television every meal, it is normal. Whether they seldom communicate, or constant dialogue is the norm, it becomes the culture, but the people in it are the least likely to be able to accurately recognize it. This also hampers the ability, at times, of veterans in an organization to alter the dynamic/culture that they have been a part of. What feels normal, even if it is not good, can be comfortable, whereas change almost always is not. If the current environment is perceived as comfortable for the people in it, they want the new people to become a part of that, not to be a threat to it.

A trend in all fields now is to talk about the culture. One of the offshoots of this is changing the culture you have or developing the culture you desire. Most of the time people are really describing climate—the current tone—rather than culture—the way we do things around here. One other factor that can be confusing is many times we use the word culture when the real word that applies is leadership.

If we have a dysfunctional culture, we probably have a dysfunctional leader. This might not apply if we have a new leader, but what we probably meant in that situation is that we *had* a dysfunctional leader—or even a series of less than stellar ones. If you ever wonder why people say the culture is bad, it might be because it may feel safer to say that than say the leader is bad. This is doubly true if you are the leader!

If you really believe it is culture rather than leadership, then ask yourself why the University of Alabama football fans were so worried when coach Nick Saban retired after developing the most successful program in the country. If it really is the culture, then him leaving wouldn't cause a ripple of concern. However, if the leader influences the culture more than the culture influences the leader, no wonder they became so worried. And realistically my guess is, over time, the culture becomes what the leader is. But you can mull that one over.

However, even if it is the leader, the effective leader recognizes the importance of the culture and intentionally works to continually make it better. Also, typically the best way to do this is indirectly. If you really want to 'Change the Culture,' two words you should never say out loud are *change* and *culture*. When a culture feels threatened, that is when it is strongest and most resistant to improvement. Subtlety is crucial when improving the culture of an organization.

One of the most common ways to change the culture is to start by changing the climate. If today, for the first time, the entire school decides to greet the students, that changes the climate. However, if the school never stops greeting the students, that changes the culture. If you change today, you change the climate. If you never change back, you change the culture.

If you change today, you change the climate. If you never change back, you change the culture.

But please remember the importance of talent on the team. I am not sure what the culture of the Chicago Bulls NBA basketball team was when they won six championships in eight years. But I do know that run stopped dramatically when Michael Jordan retired. That could be coincidence, but the same thing happened to the New England Patriots in the NFL when their all-time great quarterback, Tom Brady, went to another team. It isn't culture. You could rightly argue it isn't leadership by itself, but it's hard to argue that talent was not a critical component of their success. And maybe, one other component of talent is the ability to influence peers and impact the culture.

How can new staff members help alter the culture of an entire organization? Is that possible? How do we start? And is it possible to do so without ostracizing them and offending more established peers? Let's take a look at one idea.

Creating a Desired Subculture

The best way to start the process of improving a culture is to develop a subculture that you would like the culture to become. Whether it starts at a grade level at an elementary school, a team at a middle school, or a department at a high school, these can all be possibilities. Having one outstanding grade level gives you a chance at having all grade levels improve. If the science department at a high school can become stellar in how they share and operate, they can become the model for other departments as well as the school as an entirety. Maybe instead of a job-alike group, it is a group of three new teachers who have disparate assignments. Whatever form it takes, one of the easiest and most effective paths is to make sure at least one of the members of the new subculture is a new teacher. Remember that people who are within a culture for a lengthy period of time often are comfortable in it, even if it is dysfunctional. And, depending on their length of stay, they may not even see it as dysfunctional. One of the reasons for this is that there really isn't anything about a culture that is tangible. There is nothing that we can touch or physically feel that is culture. Culture (and climate) both really exist in people's minds. We change cultures by changing people's minds—altering the way they view their setting. That is why one of the most effective people to help assist us down a new and different path is a new and different teacher. Let's think about ways they can help this happen.

Induction Starts at the Interview

Since culture exists in people's minds, it might be a good idea to start formulating their vision as quickly as possible. A good place to start that formulation is the interview. Helping to establish the vision of a school culture is easier with a blank slate than it is with a developed perception. That is why new staff members, and their interviews, are prime opportunities.

Let's say that you would like to increase the level of professional dress in your school. This isn't suggesting you do this; it is just sharing a hypothetical approach. Say the culture for clothing choices has been more of an 'anything goes' tone than you would like in your setting. So, during the interview, a male new teaching prospect comes in and you are thinking about considering offering him a position. One question you ask is, "How often do you think you would wear a tie to work?"

What do you think this person may see as the expectations of dress in the school? Do you think it increases the likelihood that he would wear a tie on the first day? If he joined a department with five male teachers, and one of them regularly wears a tie, is there a chance we are now up to two? If the other male is highly regarded, does that make it easier for the new teacher to continue the neckwear game?

Could the same thing also happen if you hired three male teachers in a year and you asked all of them the tie question in an interview? Is there a chance they all show up the first day of school wearing ties? Is this a possible subgroup (subculture) that could possibly begin the clothing trend? You would want to reinforce their style choice by noticing and complimenting their neckwear. Other staff members may want to join the club. Now this all may seem silly, and perhaps you couldn't care less about ties. But the idea is the same in that to move the culture as a whole in a direction, a subculture is often the best place to start. When you want to move from zero to ten, many times, you have to start by going from zero to one.

When you want to move from zero to ten, many times, you have to start by going from zero to one.

Introducing During the Interview: Classroom Visitations

One way to help new teachers become more like the best teachers is to have them observe the classrooms of their outstanding peers. We will explore this more at another point in the book but I want to share it as an example now as it ties into the induction process. If the culture of the school is that teachers visiting peers' classrooms does not typically occur, then how do we begin the process?

If a principal just announces that teachers should observe each other when they can, most likely it will turn out that they never can. If the principal 'mandates' every teacher goes into two other rooms and issues a schedule, there is a good chance that, if they actually do visit, it might result in a less than positive dynamic, and the opportunity could produce resentment and hurt feelings.

If you would like to start the process of teachers visiting other classrooms, and this is a new concept to your school, you could ask a prospective candidate during the interview, "What would you think about visiting some outstanding teachers' classrooms and being able to learn from them?" Since it is an interview, and they probably want the job, they are likely to respond positively. Now in their mind, visiting classrooms must be something the school does; thus, they see that as the culture of this school. If you can get your new teachers and some (even start with one) of your best teachers to do this, then that is a subculture that can be expanded.

Assigning Mentors

The vast majority of schools assign mentors to their new staff members. In some places it is mandated, and others do it voluntarily to provide support. This is a wonderful idea and quite needed. However, like most things, it is the quality of who is involved and what and how well it is done that will determine the value. When a mentor is assigned to a new teacher, what are we telling them? Whether intended or not, what we are really implying is that this is the person you should aim to become, this is what we hope you strive to be at the pinnacle of your career. Though that might be an exaggeration, it is definitively implied in the process. Why would you ever assign a new teacher—even if they are just new to your building, not to the profession—anyone but the very best? How are mentors chosen in your state, district, or school? Sometimes we base it on seniority or who is willing. A big part of how too many mentors are chosen is by convenience.

Who has the same plan time, who has a handy room location, who teaches the same grade level, who is the same gender, age, race, and so on. We are assigning the new teacher a role model whether we title it that or not. If we want our new teachers to become like our best teachers, who should be the mentors in our setting? Clearly grade level, room location, and planning period could be a consideration, but they should never be *the* consideration. It is imperative that we intentionally connect our new staff members to our best staff members. If this is not done, then we diminish the impact our best teachers can have on a most precious commodity—our new faculty. Plus, what an opportunity we've lost to establish a subculture that can help provide a direction for our school.

> **It is imperative that we intentionally connect our new staff members to our best staff members.**

Our best teachers are always challenging the boundaries of the culture. They want to try and do things that others in the school are not. Let's make sure we give them eager groupies to join the club of visionaries that we already have in the school.

Keep in mind if you want to go from 0 to 10, the hardest step is 0 to 1. By the way, the next biggest challenge is 1 to 2. Provide some intentionality to increase the speed of this difficult but essential process.

There Is Always a Welcoming Committee

It is critical that there is intentionalness in building peer connections in any setting, including in your school. We want new students to meet positive peers who will make them feel welcome and help them meet others to befriend. Well, we never get too old for that. Make sure the mentor or a group of teachers makes a connection, invites them to sit with them at faculty meetings, tells them about the Friday happy hour and any other formal and informal opportunities in their new setting, etc. However, make sure it is the people that we want reaching out, that it is those who will provide all the assistance they need and desire.

That they work to celebrate their success—or sometimes their survival—as we all reflect on our initial-year adventures. The reason this must be thought out and the reason a positive approach is encouraged is that many schools, too many schools, have other less than positive groups that look to welcome new students and staff members.

There are probably students in many schools where we would rather not recruit the student who just moved in as their peer. They may not be the best role model or provide a positive path for their new 'friend.' Sadly, in many places this same dynamic applies to the adults who join the school.

There may be a faculty member or two (or more) that you would rather not seek to connect with the new teacher. Their attitude, effort level, and tone might not be the best direction to lead to success. I'd guess you were not trying to hire a new teacher to be negative, cynical, or think negatively about the students you serve. Well, if they join that group, they may have a tough time resisting the negative tug that now surrounds them. Subcultures are not inherently positive or negative. However, subcultures often aim to become the dominant culture in an organization, or at least they aim to increase their influence. So not only do you want to hire new teachers to build the positive, but you also want to make sure that when they join your team that it is the right part of the team. Most schools have a great majority of positive and caring people. Continue to add to that and nurture the newbies so that they help the dynamic in the setting continue to grow.

One reason you need to make sure the positive people connect with your new staff members is that the negative group is already recruiting. They have already picked out a matching shirt with the new staff member's name embroidered on it. And they cannot wait to have them try it on.

The Cost of Getting It Wrong

Always remember culture exists in our minds. We enter a new school or organization, and we are trying to figure out how to fit in. We want to please the bosses and connect with our peers.

One of the ways the culture is so impactful is that it tells us what the real rules are.

The principal at the opening faculty meeting tells us we should contact one parent with a positive call a week. You are new and want to please the boss. You ask your mentor how we get family phone numbers. Instead of getting one of the shining star teachers as a mentor, you were assigned the one next door who isn't just burnt out; they may have never been on fire in the first place. The mentor doesn't want to have you, as the newbie, show them up, so they tell you, "We don't call home here with good news. They just tell us to, but nobody does it." Well, you want to fit in, and you were assigned to 'fit in' with this person.

After a couple of weeks, one of the students is struggling with behavior and as a result academics. Since this is not a positive phone call—which they told you not to do—you ask your mentor how to get family phone numbers because you want to ask for the family's help with the struggling student. The mentor says, "We don't call parents here at all, we just email." Since culture exists in your mind, what do you start to think the culture in the school is regarding family contact? Well, obviously you are a quick learner, so you might begin with what your mentor said everybody in the school does.

You have a faculty, grade level, or department meeting and someone shares an expectation. You are ready to please, but the mentor tells you after the meeting: Here is what you should do instead. Your mentor and others in your hallway wear jeans every day, but the principal asked people to only do so on Fridays. Your mentor says everyone wears jeans though it is against the rules because the administration is too scared and lazy to deal with it. And to show they are correct, they tell you to notice the garb of the two teachers across the hall who share the same viewpoint.

In the teachers' lounge, you hear—at first as a murmur, and as the year transpires as an increasingly steady drumbeat—that the parents here don't care like they should, students are different than they used to be, and we wish it were like the good old days. You are young enough that to you they must mean the times before Beyoncé released a country album, but those were good old days as well.

The culture does not want to change. And the only people who want the culture to change are the best people. And they even know a path forward. But what they need is support, colleagues, and others who also want to improve the school and even the district. They are willing to work for it. But they need some peers to join them on the journey. These people must be mentors. They must be the ones to help lead the subculture; they have to have energetic recruits. We will explore more about intentionality, but this is too valuable of an opportunity to pass up.

Make sure the good guys win. Trust me they can, because you have just added someone who is made for this and who wants to help steer the crew in the right direction. After all, that is why they joined your school.

7

Improve *the* Pool and *Our* Pool
Student Teaching

When I outlined this book, I felt that the topic of student teaching was essential. It is critical at the macro level (the profession) and the micro level (your school and the future classroom of students). I just wasn't sure where to place it. It seems like it should be before hiring, interviewing, and induction, yet it isn't just limited to your school or any one school. Instead, it impacts every school and each person who student-teaches, and future teachers. It really is central to helping all teachers become like the best teachers. But it is also a separate category to any other part of the book. Yet the strategic thinking and understanding involved in this chapter are essential to everything we do to help all teachers become exceptional, so, here it is.

The Macro View

I realize that with many current nontraditional or alternate paths to teaching, many people do not have a traditional 8-, 12-, or 16-week student teaching experience, where they are assigned to work with someone on a full-time regular basis as the culminating experience

DOI: 10.4324/9781003492535-9

that is part of their four-year college program. However, many students still do take the more traditional student teaching path. Additionally, the nontraditional programs can require some level of observations, co-teaching, and possibly a different type of 'student teaching' experience to gain a teaching license. Whatever the structure may be, the same principles apply. But to make it have a better flow for the reader, I am going to describe a more traditional student teaching experience and have faith you can apply the ideas to the alternative structures that are part of your setting. The reason I called this a macro view is that when you have a student teacher in your school, they may not actually end up teaching in your school. They may be in your school because you are close to their university or their hometown, or just because you are kind enough to host them and support their career and the profession. The reason they are there is irrelevant; you provide them with the experience they need to help maximize their talents and put them on the path to excellence.

In the previous chapter I described how mentors are most often assigned, and that in many settings, it is done by convenience. It is done by who volunteers to take them, who has a similar teaching assignment, plan time, etc. Not only is this a potential disservice to the new teacher, but it is also a direct disservice to your students and school, and to the education community depending on where they end up teaching. Or not teaching. This person is joining your school or a school, so you want them to head toward excellence. Thus, you need to make sure they are mentored by the very best people.

Whatever a building mentor provides or doesn't provide may be minimal compared to the student teaching experience. Once again, how are many student teacher placements determined in a school? Who among your staff will volunteer to take them or what grade level or subject would they prefer? Yep, these are factors but not the important factor. The determination should be based on the quality of the hosting teacher in your school. That is, the teacher who they will be student teaching with. We might want to sacrifice convenience for an exponentially increased importance.

The Career Impact

The role of the host teacher is essential. And the only teachers that should serve as host teachers are outstanding teachers in a school. Ponder this:

> If an average student teacher teaches with the best teacher in a school, in two weeks, who do they start to talk like? The best teacher.
>
> If an average student teacher teaches with the best teacher in a school, in six weeks, who do they start to dress like? The best teacher.

If an average student teacher teaches with the best teacher in a school, in 12 weeks, who do they start to teach like?

And, most importantly, if an average student teacher teaches with the best teacher in a school, in 12 weeks, who do they start to teach like? The best teacher.

You want to know something else that is amazing? In two years, who does that former student teacher, who now teaches professionally, talk like, dress like, and teach like? That best teacher they student-taught with. Why do they continue to do this? Because it works. What they learned from that teacher works, so they continue using them as a role model. Of course, they infuse their own personality, flair, dress code, and style, but throughout their career they reflect on, 'What would the teacher I student-taught with do in this situation?'

And, if you ever wonder about the importance of who they student-teach with, ask yourself this:

> If an average student teacher teaches with an average teacher in a school, in two weeks, who do they start to talk like? In six weeks, who do they dress like? In 12 weeks, who do they start to teach like?

And the challenge is, when they have their own classroom, they will reflect back on an experience that isn't as likely to have shown them how to successfully work with the most challenging students, how to establish and maintain a tone of voice that they want to implement every day, and how to stay positive with colleagues who do not. Let's go one more step further, or is it lower?

> If an average student teacher teaches with a below-average teacher in a school, in two weeks, who do they start to talk like? In six weeks, who do they dress like? In 12 weeks, who do they start to teach like?

What is even more worrisome? If an impressionable future educator student-teaches with a below-average professional, we may ruin their career. Or at the very least make it much more challenging. They may not see the value of teaching, they may enter the profession with a negative mindset, and they may feel that it's okay to yell at students since they saw a seasoned professional do that while student teaching. Or they decide teaching is not their choice of a life journey. The ineffective teacher may not be liked, respected, or capable of managing a classroom. Additionally, they may not even like teaching or the students in their classroom. You are new, and they have experience. Why would you want to head down their path?

The Micro View

This view is more understandable and more selfish. Instead of the global view of helping education, let's see how you can help yourself.

You know why you should want to make sure every student teacher you have in your school works with an outstanding teacher? Because you may hire them. If there is a teacher shortage or even if there is not a shortage and you have a student teacher, I feel like the chances of them ending up in your school are higher than a random candidate. Additionally, the better the leader is and the better their student teaching experience is, the better the chances of them wanting to remain in your school once their career starts. Why would you not want them to develop into the best teacher they can, as quickly as possible?

One other benefit. The subculture. If you link a great teacher with a (now after student teaching with the best) dynamic new teacher, that is an inherent subculture. You have two people who are likely to now have a similar view of education, a comparable care level for the students, and a love for the school. They already have a professional relationship and possibly on some level a personal relationship. The host teacher may have already connected their student teacher with the 'right' people in the school to continue to expand this dynamic in your school. Their closest colleague in the school is likely to be exceptional and would love to add someone who has the same belief system as they and the host teacher do.

Remember, going from 1 to 2 is easier than 0 to 1. But do you know what is even easier? Going from 2 to 3.

We owe it to every student teacher to provide them with the most guidance and support. We owe it to them; we owe it to the profession, regardless of where they end up; and we always, always, owe it to the students they will serve no matter the location. If there are students in the classroom, they deserve a high-quality, caring teacher in there with them.

> **We owe it to every student teacher to provide them with the most guidance and support.**

Part III

Improving the Teachers We Have

8

Teaching the Teachers

Coaches generally have two ways to improve their athletic teams: Add better players and improve the players they have. They could buy nice uniforms, get better equipment, or come up with a catchier team motto. Adding these things has little downside. Better uniforms may be a first step to team pride. Better equipment could help the skill level or performance. And who doesn't want a fun team motto?! But unfortunately, things like this usually have little or no significant upside. However, if it makes the players more excited about being on the team, that is great. If the uniforms attract more talented players to join, that is a clear plus. But why do these things matter? Because they either allow you to add more talented players or increase the quality of players you have by figuring out a way for them to try harder or be more confident.

In Chapter 2 we explored an example about flexible seating—a current trend in education. We realized that flexible seating is not the determinant of teacher quality. Rather, teacher quality is the determinant of whether flexible seating will be beneficial in a particular classroom or setting. But if a teacher is excited about implementing flexible seating in their classroom, then the principal needs to be highly supportive of them doing so. Why? Because if the teacher is more excited about teaching, the students are likely to be more excited about learning. Alternative furniture will not

DOI: 10.4324/9781003492535-11

alone increase teaching and learning in the classroom. Of that I am confident. I am also equally confident that the enthusiasm of the teacher is a determinant of their success in the classroom.

That is why things like staff polo shirts, donuts in the teachers' lounge, and catchy slogans can be positive. They also can be neutral. They also can be negative. If the culture in the school—and the aura around the principal—is negative, donuts in the teachers' lounge can make people mad, leading them to ask why there isn't fruit instead. Maybe some staff will even complain that something is wrong with their donut because it has a hole in it.

If the dynamic is good, staff polo shirts can be beneficial as it makes you feel like part of a team. However, if the tone in the school is such that negativity rules, people can be angry that the shirt color doesn't match their eyes, and this may not be a team good people want to join. Please remember these ideas are neither good nor bad. They are neither the problems nor the solutions. Instead, let's look at things that can actually be the solutions to the problems.

The Limits of Induction and Onboarding

In most organizations, induction and even onboarding are really centered around 'following the rules' and 'learning the ropes.' Here is where you park, this is your mailbox, locating the restrooms, and so on. They can also assist with paperwork, when grades are due, the IEP process for special education students, etc. These are positive and necessary things. This guidance can help you avoid being embarrassed and help a newcomer to not feel lost. That is great. However, often they do not include moving beyond rules and procedures to effective classroom practices. We need to help new teachers become exceptional classroom managers, and they need to be highly effective and dynamic in the area of instruction. This is the real road to becoming an outstanding teacher—the best of the best.

Often, induction is built for the convenience of others rather than for the development of new staff. Half of the first day may be specifically designed for new staff on insurance because the insurance rep is there, or someone at central office would like to check it off their list. Insurance is important, but that 22-year-old teacher is wondering how to set up their physical classroom or what procedures they should establish for the first day of school. The best learning happens when it is provided when needed. No reason to talk about parent teacher conferences at the start of the year—especially with new staff. They may feel overwhelmed, and it will add to their stress level. Plus, they may not know what you are talking about. However, the week before parent teacher conferences happen, there is a good chance that they are desiring specific direction. Doing things when they are needed is more productive than doing them when there is time. Some things help certain people and others can benefit everyone. Let's get started on improving the teachers that are currently in our schools.

> **Doing things when they are needed is more productive than doing them when there is time.**

Teaching Versus Telling

We do so much 'telling' in education it is incredible. We get told to raise our test scores, we get told to improve our attitude, we get told to improve our classroom management. The first time we hear this, it causes us to sit up straighter and try the same things we are doing or try them harder. It is sort of like speeding down a highway and seeing a speed trap. We change our behavior and pretend that we are attempting to do the right thing. But being honest, most of us check the rearview mirror once we pass the patrolman and then resume the previous brisk pace. And if we do get pulled over, we are tempted to point out others who were going faster than us who were not caught. Nothing is different, but we either temporarily improved our effort, or we are ticked off at being picked on.

Let's look at a school example. Have you or do you know anyone who has been told, "Raise your test scores!" My guess is yes, but even if you haven't you can probably imagine that many educators have in recent years. With that in mind, do you know anyone who has been intentionally holding back on

raising their test scores? Does it seem likely that many educators try to keep a little slack in the line when they are trying
to improve their scores? Not only does that seem silly, but it is
actually ridiculous, offensive, or both. Everyone has their test
scores up as high as they know how to get them. Do you know
why? Do you know who it most benefits? It benefits them. It
benefits the educator themselves. That is how we can be assured
everyone in education is doing the best they know how in this
area. Even people who do not believe in testing and/or people
who are not particularly skilled have their test scores up as high
as they know how.

It reminds me of a former track coach at my school when I
was a principal. She used to yell at her runners every day. She
always shouted, "Run faster!" I used to share with her that my
guess is they are running about as fast as they know how. If
they knew how to run faster, they would because it benefits
them. Telling them to run faster probably has a limited return
value. It is sort of like the highway patrol story. They may react
temporarily, and the reaction could actually be counterproduc-
tive, due to a loss of personal confidence or diminished credibility from the coach. Especially if it becomes a regular chant.
However, if you taught them to run faster, that might be more
likely to work. And it might be more likely to work for a more
extended period of time than telling them. So why don't we
try a differing approach? The 'old-school' way has not been
too effective.

Why Don't We Teach Instead of Tell?

Let's reflect for a minute. Why don't leaders teach more and tell
less? It seems like they should, as it benefits them as well. And
that is true for leaders at every level. See if you can answer these
questions. Hint, they may form a pattern.

> Why doesn't a state department teach the leaders of struggling
> school districts or challenged schools how to raise their test
> scores?

Why doesn't a superintendent teach their principals how to increase their student performance?

Why doesn't a principal teach their teachers how to increase their students' academic performance?

I'd guess by now you have figured out that these three questions all have one similar answer. They don't know how. This isn't a dig or a slight. It is the truth, though. The reason we know they don't know how is that they would benefit by doing these things. If a state department knew how to raise test scores, they would teach districts and schools because it would not only make the districts and schools shine; it would make the state department look good as well! If the superintendent could teach their principals how to increase their student performance, it would make the superintendent become a superstar. And if the principal could teach their teachers how to increase performance, everyone benefits—students, teachers, and administrators.

Another reason is that it really is difficult to teach someone something that is really difficult. It is a challenge to run really fast in track, or we would all be Olympians or at least finish in the top three in the conference meet. It is hard to increase test scores in any school, much less one with a higher-need population. So, what should we do? The first thing is to start where we can make a difference. Remember the teacher who opened their computer on the first day of school and only 11 of their 25 students were in attendance? The teacher impacted who and what they could. Then they worked on the next challenge. Let's try to find something we can teach that would impact things that are more difficult to achieve.

Classroom Management

Classroom management is a timeless issue. It never goes away because working with young people as well as older people always has challenges and surprises. There also seems to be an increase in the need to build skills in this area since the pandemic. The isolated time for students may have decreased their academic levels while increasing their behavioral challenges. But regardless of cause and effect or even trendline in student behavior, this area has been and continues to be one that hurts student performance and hampers teacher retention.

Though the pandemic had a significant influence on many things, including schools, there are some things that haven't changed. Before the pandemic, two of the biggest reasons teachers left their school or even the profession were they didn't like their supervisor (principal) and/or they were not successful in managing their classroom. As you know, the pandemic changed everything, well almost everything.

Following the pandemic, two of the biggest reasons teachers left their school or even the profession were they didn't like their supervisor (principal) and/or they were not successful in managing their classroom. I guess not everything was different after all. So, with that in mind, what is something we could teach that would help all teachers to be like the best teachers and increase the quality and quantity of teachers in the profession and in your setting? How about beginning the journey of teaching by centering on classroom management? Well, to you that might seem old school. But I'd like to ask a couple of questions.

1. What percent of teachers in your school (or any school, anywhere) would like their job better if they were better at classroom management?
2. What percent of teachers in your school (or any school, anywhere) would like their job better if they were **significantly better** at classroom management?

The answer to Question 1 is easy: 100%. If any educator could get their students to behave better, they would get their students to behave better. How do we know this? Because classroom management is selfish. If any of us could get the students to behave better, we would, if for no other reason than it makes our jobs better. Sure, it would increase learning, etc., but let's be honest, we'd like our job better if the students were more cooperative.

> **If any educator could get their students to behave better, they would get their students to behave better.**

Question 2 is a little trickier because every school is different and everyone's opinion about the thoughts, views, and wishes of their colleagues varies as well. The difference in the questions of course is the term *significantly better*. That probably means it is not everyone because your best teachers may not have room to be significantly better. When I ask teachers, principals, and superintendents, they usually respond with anywhere from 60 to 95 percent. Your school may vary, and your opinion may as well. However, it seems that it is a significant group size that would like their job better and probably feel more effective as a teacher if they were better at managing the students.

Now let's go a little further down the logic trail:

What do you think principals would be more likely to be effective at: a) teaching teachers to *raise their test scores* or b) teaching teachers to *improve their classroom management*? That's an easy one: b. Teaching teachers to manage their classroom more effectively. We probably all agree on that.

Next question: Point your thumb up or down. What do you think would happen to *test scores* in general if we were able to help teachers be more effective at managing their classrooms? I am guessing that is a thumbs up.

Next question: Point your thumb up or down. What do you think would happen to *teacher morale* in general if we were able to help all teachers be more effective at managing their classrooms? I am guessing that is a thumbs up.

Next question: Point your thumb up or down. What do you think would happen to *teacher retention* if we were able to help all teachers be more effective at managing their classrooms? I am guessing that is a thumbs up—we are on a roll.

Next question: Point your thumb up or down. What do you think would happen to *principal morale* in general if we were able to help all teachers be more effective at managing their classrooms? I am guessing that is a thumbs up as well.

So, it seems like we have come to the conclusion that if leaders could help teachers improve their classroom management, the benefits would be far and wide. Test scores would go up, morale would go up for teachers and leaders, and retention would get a boost. And just think of the double benefit if the principal could assist with improving classroom management. The teachers may even like them better! Like Michael Scott said in *The Office* television show, "Win-win-win-win." Now I am not going to tell you to do this as that would be disingenuous. Instead, let's see if we can teach you how to do it.

9

The Specificity of Teaching Classroom Management

Picture a mom with her young children at a grocery store. She is attempting to shop while simultaneously working to keep a handle on her kids. They are good kids, but they are active kids. A complete stranger sees this and tells her to get her children to behave better. She would probably respond with an angry look or mama bear claws ready. Or possibly she would feel shame, whether she should or not. After that, she is not better at managing her kids and is actually in a worse emotional state than she was before, and possibly less capable of corralling her crew successfully. There are lots of reasons the stranger's comment didn't help, but one of them is that the mom was doing the best she knew how. For sure if a parent could get their children to behave better—at home or in public—they would. If for no other reason than because it benefits them.

Now, picture the same scenario, only the stranger somehow makes a suggestion that actually helps the mom manage her children's behavior better. Amazing! The mom might actually follow the stranger like a pied piper in case they had any more tips to share. This fictional tale helps us understand how teachers are receptive to improving if it helps their practice. And classroom management is a great place to start.

DOI: 10.4324/9781003492535-12

The Specifics Are the Difference Makers

When a basketball coach is attempting to help one of their players with shooting a jump shot, they have lots of options. They can tell them to hold their elbow in, they can suggest they look at the rim, they can suggest they should land in the same spot that they take off from. None of these are wrong, and they are common tips. However, some players have such a sense of self that they can self-monitor and even regulate that. But sadly, many others have an inaccurate self-image. They think their elbow is in, they feel they are landing in the same spot, but that may not be correct. Placing a piece of tape on the floor or providing video may assist with the self-check process.

Teaching has so many things going on that it is difficult to self-monitor. However, teaching specific things that a teacher can be aware of that they are doing or not doing can be very beneficial. Once we understand specific things the best teachers have in common, then it becomes possible to share them with everyone.

> Once we understand specific things the best teachers have in common, then it becomes possible to share them with everyone.

Clip Charts: The Problem or the Solution?

I am sure there are many groans just from me sharing those two words. You may not like clip charts, or you think they should be banned, outlawed, or illegal! I will not debate you, but I'd like to share an example using clip charts that may increase an understanding of classroom management practices that can be shared and taught.

Just so we are all on the same page, in an elementary class a clip chart is a large sheet of paper posted somewhere in the room that has every student's name on it and is visible to everyone in the room. Next to each name is a colorful clothes pin or paper-clip that the teachers move down when a student misbehaves or move up when a student self-corrects for a period of time or does something positive. It is like ClassDojo, or any type of assertive discipline that can be used for positive and negative behavior.

In a secondary classroom there may be multiple charts. One for the first hour, one for the second, etc. Ironically, there are outstanding teachers that successfully use clip charts at the secondary level and less effective colleagues who unsuccessfully use clip charts in the room next door.

Now before you throw this book away, I want to revisit a way of thinking. Clip charts are not the problem, and clip charts are not the solution. Do you know what is amazing? Clip charts work in a great teacher's classroom. You know what else is amazing? Clip charts are ineffective in an ineffective teacher's classroom. Remind me, what is the variable? Oh, that's right, the teacher.

One of the criticisms of clip charts is that they may humiliate the students. I don't totally disagree, but if a great teacher can use them effectively and an ineffective teacher cannot, what is not the deciding factor? The clip chart is not; the teacher is. If you feel that the clip chart is the humiliator, I'd like you to think about how many years it would take before a great teacher who uses clip charts starts humiliating their students. The answer, as we all know, is that they would never do that. No matter what assertive discipline—or any management—approach they use, they will never humiliate students. Never. However, you are thinking, "What about the ineffective teachers who use clip charts? They humiliate and embarrass students on a too frequent basis!" I concur completely. However, the only way to determine cause and effect is to go into an ineffective teacher's classroom who uses clip charts and humiliates their students and remove the clip chart immediately. What will the ineffective teacher continue to do until we teach them effective practices? They will continue to humiliate the students. We need to improve the person rather than eliminate the program. Especially a program that works for effective people and doesn't for others. Why would we take that away from them? If it works well for a highly successful staff member and they have great connections with students, why would we remove the practice and keep the person who is not successful with the same practice?

We shouldn't outlaw flexible seating for all just because some teachers who have trouble managing their students in desks and rows have trouble with student behavior when they go to an alternative seating approach. We also should not mandate flexible seating for a teacher who is exceptional with a more traditional room arrangement. We must use a scalpel, not a sledgehammer. Isn't that what the best teachers do with their students? It's never one size fits all. However, there are practices that are much more common in the best teachers' classrooms and almost nonexistent in those on the other end of the quality spectrum. Let's teach those to everyone. So, let's take off our biased lens toward clip charts so we can help everyone get better.

When a Student Misbehaves

There are no absolutes in classroom management, and I do not want to pretend there are. Every situation is different, every teacher is different, and the make-up of the class can vary dramatically. But there may be some specific universal teachings that can help everyone if applied to their personal practices. So, let's get started.

I would like you to reflect on this question:

> When a student misbehaves in a great teacher's classroom who uses clip charts, what does this outstanding teacher do the second the student misbehaves?

Your first instinct might be to give them the eye, go over the rules, clip them down, use proximity, redirect, point out students who are doing things correctly, threaten to clip them down, threaten to send them to the office, etc. There are a multitude of possibilities.

And to help you out, I am going to give you two hints:

1. The majority of great teachers who use clip charts do the exact same thing.
2. The majority of great teachers who do not use clip charts do the exact same thing.

So, your fears can be eliminated, since we realize the answer has nothing to do with clip charts. One of the first instincts of an outstanding teacher when a student misbehaves is to—drumroll please—keep teaching. The first instinct of outstanding classroom managers is to keep teaching for two reasons.

One is so they have a chance to keep thinking. They are going through a) all of the alternatives they can choose from (give them the eye, clip them down, redirect, etc.) and b) all of the situational factors they are dealing with—what student is it, what day of the week is it, what time of day is it, is the student's behavior trending up or trending down, when was the last vacation, when is the next vacation ... For some outstanding teachers that takes 5 seconds, for others it takes five minutes, but for both teachers they think before they react. They do not try to out quick the students. They try to out think the students. The situation matters. If it is the day before the winter break and there are five minutes left in the school day, they are not going to clip the student down. They'd be more likely to give them a cigarette and let them smoke their way to break. Obviously, that is an attempt at humor, but hopefully the concept comes through.

Two is that they realize that the student who is misbehaving is the least important student at that moment. This is not a cruel view. This is not cold-hearted or mean-spirited in any way. It is actually the opposite. If the teacher has 25 students and 24 students are behaving, why would you punish the majority for doing the right thing by ignoring them and putting the focus on the disruptor? If you have 24 students doing the right thing while one chooses not to, your biggest concern may not be, how do I get back to 25? Maybe it should be, how do I keep it from becoming 23?

And, in addition to continuing to teach, the most outstanding classroom managers also work to avoid looking at the student while they are behaving inappropriately. Once we understand the main causes of misbehavior, this will help us understand the power of *seemingly* ignoring the behavior. The two biggest causes of misbehavior are wanting Attention and wanting Power. There are a variety of percentages given, but they are usually around 90/10. In other words, estimates are that 90 percent of time when a student misbehaves, they are seeking attention and around 10 percent of the time they are seeking or guarding power. Revenge and inadequacy are sometimes separated, but for our purposes let's put them under the power category. Also, realize that students who are exceptionally good at disrupting class are also exceptionally good at disrupting the teacher and disrupting the teaching. Seldom do people repeat a behavior without a reward, and they are working to be rewarded. An important side note, what are the most likely causes of adult misbehavior? Maybe not surprisingly, they also want attention and power. Major blowups happen in schools most often when the students who are seeking power cross paths with the adults who are seeking power. They are both battling over the same space and neither wants to let go.

When a student misbehaves, the vast majority of teachers who struggle with classroom management have two primary reactions. One is to stop teaching and the other is to turn and look at the student. Well, let's think about this. Most of the time the student is misbehaving because they are seeking what? Attention. When the typical teacher stops teaching and turns and looks/stares at the student, what are they giving them? Attention. They are giving the student the reward they wanted. And then some educators talk about 'Kids today.' Well, handling this wrong didn't work with students in the past either.

Adult Behavior

If we want to improve student behavior, we have to first change adult behavior. Let's break down the previous example. If there are 25 students in class, there is a chance only some of their peers even noticed the student's inappropriate actions. So, they were receiving attention from say five students. But when the teacher stopped teaching and turned to stare at the student? Now they were getting a reward from the teacher, and thanks to the educator's assistance they now were holding an audience with every one of their classmates. This is the opposite of what we hope to have happen. Let's look at a couple of reactionary practices that work when you use them appropriately and lead to a negligible or negative result when you do not. And they are all completely up to the adult in the room.

If we want to improve student behavior, we have to first change adult behavior.

Redirect

One of the most common classroom management techniques used by almost all teachers is the redirect. Teachers redirect when they are hoping to change the course of a student's action by moving them from disrupting actions to focus on an appropriate task or behavior. Once again, redirect works great in a great teacher's room, average in an average teacher's room, and ineffectively at best, escalating at worst, in an ineffective teacher's classroom.

The most common redirect is what we described earlier: A student is misbehaving, and the teacher stops teaching and turns to look at the student and often calls their name. They pause, turn to the student, and say something like, "What do you think, Kevin?" Instantly the student becomes the center of attention in the class, which is the opposite of what we were hoping to accomplish. Instead, what the best teachers do is embed their redirect into their classroom management practices. They do this by including more than one student when a student is behaving inappropriately and utilize this practice on a regular basis when students are behaving appropriately, so that it is not just utilized for misbehavior, which is how the students know to look up and check out who it is that is misbehaving. I call it handing attention to them on a platter. At least make them earn it. Let's look at an example of embedding redirection.

Embedding Redirection

Embedded classroom management is not an event. It is part of the natural flow of the classroom. The event of a student misbehaving is a disruption to learning. The event of a teacher dealing with the student misbehaving incorrectly is also a disruption to learning.

The earlier example, when Kevin is being inappropriate and the teacher stops, looks at him and says, "What do you think, Kevin?" is clearly made up of two events: Kevin's behavior and the teacher's response. Now the tone and delivery of the teacher is also very significant. If the teacher says it in a way that seems like the natural flow of the classroom—because they regularly call on a wide variety of students in this manner to keep energy and attention—potentially learning does not stop. But if even in a minor way the teacher has a twinge of negativity, it can be disruptive. However, in a natural flow, the teacher does not stop and stare; instead, the teacher wants to keep up energy rather than have it come to a halt.

Another alternative is if Kevin is sitting by Amber and Dewayne. Rather than singling out Kevin to redirect him, the teacher engagingly says, "Any thoughts Amber, Dewayne, Kevin?" And then quickly follows up with another part of the room, adding, "Anyone over here Isaiah, Caleb, Brittany?" Kevin was the only one that was not behaving correctly, but by embedding his name in a series with students who were doing the right thing, it pulls Kevin in without rewarding him with attention. The teacher can also do this without stopping the flow of the class and not even looking at the student.

But to make this highly effective, a teacher needs to do this on a regular basis in their classroom when things are going well so that it is part of the natural rhythm when redirecting a student. What happens in too many classes is that the teacher's first instinct is to stop and give the student attention. An even more escalating behavior is when the teacher stops, looks at the culprit, and then says something attacking like, "Would you like to take the chalk and teach?!" Or turns to a group who are conversing inappropriately and chirps, "Do you two have something you'd like to say to the class?" or "Is what you have to say more important than what I have to say?" Regardless of whether we call this redirecting, it is definitively escalating.

All teachers redirect. The best ones embed redirection into their teaching so it can be utilized when needed to improve behavior. Let's look at one more example in the next chapter that not all teachers use as part of their approach.

10

The Power of Proximity

Many excellent and many average teachers use proximity. Few ineffective teachers use proximity. Proximity is physically moving closer to a student and is often used to correct or eliminate misbehavior. When a teacher moves closer, it hopefully increases the chances of a student self-correcting and allows the teacher to communicate verbally or nonverbally in a less disrupting and more precise manner.

Rather than calling out a student's name to get them redirected, quite often moving closer to them, putting your hand on their shoulder, or even just standing near them has the same result. The difference is that it does add to the gift of attention and may be more likely to avoid a power struggle. If a student is tapping their pencil and it seems to be distracting to those around them, a teacher who is stationary could say, "Michelle, please quit tapping your pencil." Now, we may not know if the students around Michelle noticed the pencil tapping, but there is a pretty good chance that multiple students, regardless of their location, just became aware of the teacher's comment. If the teacher says it nicely and quietly, it is less noticeable, but if that was replaced with proximity, the audience can be reduced to one—Michelle.

When standing next to them, the teacher could very gently touch their shoulder, place their hand lightly on the tapping hand

DOI: 10.4324/9781003492535-13

or the pencil, or if needed, quickly lean down and whisper to the student. This seems like common sense. And it sort of is. But for it to truly be effective, a teacher must infuse proximity into their classroom on a regular basis.

If the teacher regularly walks around to all parts of the room and passes near all students, it becomes ingrained in the culture or norm of the class. Just by walking around, it prevents or reduces potential disruptions from the students. Additionally, it allows the teacher—seemingly coincidentally—to be near a particular student at the particular time they need to be there. It is not an event and does not provide the student with the attention they may have been seeking. The teacher being there is so normal because they are near each student in class on a frequent basis.

Leaving for Lunch

Recently, I had a high school teacher ask for guidance with about two weeks left in the school year. He shared that his fourth-hour class is to leave for lunch at 11:39. (Sidenote: isn't it weird that in schools lunches are seldom normal times like 11:45?) Anyhow, he said they have started getting up on their own and walking out the door at 11:37, and he wondered if I had any suggestions on how to get this to stop. I shared that I had some ideas that would work for the last two weeks of the school year. But my real concern was, how did this ever start? And particularly, how did it get to the point that the entire class joins the club of wrongdoing?

What happened in that class the first time the first student left early? Well, you could chase the student down, send them to the office, give them a consequence, etc. But what I really wanted to know was, what could the teacher do to reduce the likelihood of that behavior happening again? Maybe a detention was the answer and there are no more concerns. Maybe. But let's think about what the teacher may do the next day to lower the odds of a repeat performance.

He was in a group, and we were just talking about proximity. So, I asked him this: "Regardless of how you handled the first day, where are two locations you could 'coincidentally' be at 11:36 the next day to reduce the likelihood of him bolting for lunch early?"

Any guesses? Of course, you know if at 11:36 you seemingly by random chance end up standing next to the student, that probably diminishes the chances of him getting up and walking out early. The other option? 'Coincidentally' being by the door. That also makes it less likely he would bull rush to the cafeteria. But it is also critical that if you are standing by the door, it must seem natural and not like a dare on your part for him to 'try it.' Don't act like a giant nutcracker holding a bayonet. Teach your teachers to embed movement into teaching so that they can be where they need to be exactly when they need to be there. If you use proximity today, it changes the climate. If you embed proximity into your teaching regularly, it becomes the culture. It takes a regular rhythm to accomplish your purpose. A person doesn't lose weight starving themselves one day and loading up on cookies the next. It is about consistently doing the correct thing, so it is in your repertoire when needed.

> **It is about consistently doing the correct thing, so it is in your repertoire when needed.**

The Best Teachers Do Not Try to 'Prove Who Is in Charge'

The best piece of advice I received in education as a teacher and as a principal was, "You don't have to prove who is in charge; everybody knows who is in charge. And the more you try to prove it, the more people try to prove you wrong." How often does the best teacher try to prove who is in charge? Never; everybody already knows it. Conversely, how often does a struggling teacher try to prove who is in charge? It seems like 10 times every hour, and there are constantly 20 students trying to prove them wrong. And the students usually have great success doing so.

However, if a teacher student-taught with a teacher who tried to prove who is in charge, or was mentored by someone who liked to talk tough, how would they know what is right and what is wrong? This is why those experiences are so important. But if they did not learn what is correct, then we must teach them what is correct now. It goes beyond modeling, and it is essential to be very specific.

Power Versus Influence

I've also learned that in education, none of us have power. We may wish we did, but we don't. Principals do not have power and neither do superintendents, and I am not outing anyone here. If they were honest, they would acknowledge that as fact. This is not to be discouraging because the thing they do have—at least the good ones do—is influence. The best ones know it and utilize it. See, power and influence are very different. In a school or district, every time we use power, we lose power. It is a finite resource that is limited in quantity and effectiveness. That's the bad news. The good news is that influence can be unlimited. See, every time we use influence correctly, we actually garner more influence.

> **Every time we use influence correctly, we actually garner more influence.**

When we use redirect correctly, we gain influence. Students are more attentive, more interested, and less distracted. When we use redirect incorrectly—usually by trying to gain power—our influence shine quickly starts to diminish.

These principals must be taught to understand how the very best people approach their classrooms. Otherwise, we rely on ineffective practices of below-average people, and then we become less than successful and more than a little frustrated.

When we let go of the lurch for power, we enable room for other tactics that exceptional educators have in abundance. When we release the power urge, we can become more reliant on ignoring. If we don't have to 'prove' who is in charge, then we can become in charge of ourselves.

If you have ever gone on a long car trip with children, or a car trip that seemed long with children, you know that the ability to ignore is essential. As you are backing down your driveway and one of the children asks, "How much farther is it?" you have no legal obligation to respond. And, if you do respond in any way—especially if it is lacquered in frustration—you encourage the behavior to be repeated. Ignoring means you have no response. No sighing, no rolling the eyes, and especially not announcing "I am ignoring you!" That is the very definition of ridiculous.

If you have the ability to control yourself, you have the ability to ignore. Without this self-control, your attempts to redirect are more likely to become power battles or at least wrongly feed the attention seekers.

> **If you have the ability to control yourself, you have the ability to ignore.**

Future Versus Past

One other essential to teach educators so they can become like the best teachers is to understand the goals of the very best teachers. When a student misbehaves in an outstanding teacher's classroom, the goal of this teacher is prevention; they want it to not happen again. When a student misbehaves in an ineffective teacher's classroom, the desire of this teacher is too often revenge. They are angry so they want the student to be upset. The teacher is embarrassed, so they want the student to be humiliated. In every situation between a teacher and a student, we need at least one adult, and it tends to work best when that adult is the teacher.

These things may seem to be common sense. And, maybe, when we are not overly caught up in the moment, I guess it may be common. But when we are tired, and it is a tough time of year, maybe some of these things we should be doing become much less common. Though if a person did not have an outstanding host teacher when student teaching or an exemplary mentor, maybe it isn't common for them at all.

Think of it as the windshield versus the rearview mirror. The best teachers generally focus on future behavior, which the students can change. And many others focus on past behavior, which has already occurred. This does not mean great teachers never see past behavior as a teachable moment. They just understand it is only used to try to help lead students to a different action and outcome in the future. Prevention versus revenge. Just like the scenario on the first day of teaching in the pandemic and

11 of 25 students showed up. The great teachers focus on what they can influence—the 11 students who were there, whereas less effective people immediately prioritize what they cannot impact. Future behavior versus past behavior of students follows this same path. We both want it not to happen again. And for sure the student can and should work on that.

The Clip Chart Conclusion

I want to get back to how all these things apply to the clip chart example. In Ms. Smith's classroom, a great teacher who uses a clip chart, her first response to misbehavior is to keep teaching. This allows her to keep thinking: What should she do with this student, Marcus, at this time of the day, on this day of the week, etc.? There is no hurry. She realizes there is no reason to out quick. She is the teacher. She is the decision maker. The student will still be there in five seconds and in five minutes. She is thinking of all the possibilities—redirect, ignore, proximity, clip him down, private conversation, and so on. Let's say she decides that it is only Tuesday, Marcus's behavior has been trending down, he has exhausted his warnings and second chances, so she is going to move his clip down.

The decision has been made. Marcus has reached the point in his behavior that Ms. Smith is going to clip him down. Who is the only person in the room that knows she is going to clip him down? Ms. Smith, the teacher. No one else knows. Also, who decides the exact moment that she is going to do the physical act of clipping him down? Ms. Smith, the teacher. Why am I emphasizing this? Because it helps us realize how exceptional classroom self-managers can effectively use clip charts and others cannot. Ms. Smith knows she is going to clip Marcus down. However, 24 students are still engaged in learning. Ms. Smith knows that and does not want to have it reach 23, 22, and below, so she keeps teaching. While teaching, she always uses proximity and thus is mobile. She knows she is going to clip Marcus down when she is ready, not based on anyone else's schedule.

Ms. Smith walks around the room at her regular pace, something she regularly embeds into her teaching. She walks to the very back of the room, behind all the students. No one responds because she meanders regularly—so often that it is part of the classroom culture. Only today, when she gets to the rear of the room, she glances at the clip chart on the front wall. She notes to herself that Marcus is the third one on the chart and he has a purple clip. Ms. Smith continues her routine regular stroll and walks by the chart. No one reacts because she regularly walks by the chart. And she doesn't clip Marcus down. Do you know why? Because 24 students are still engaged, and she is not at a natural transition point in her lesson. She actually walks by it again and takes no action toward the chart. Finally, on her third trip she is between learning points in the class. This time as she drifts by the chart naturally, she pauses at the chart and clips Marcus down in a way most teachers have never done in their careers. She reaches up and does not look at the student and does not look at the chart and clips him down and continues her circuitous route. Who is the only student that is impacted in the class? Marcus. And he is the only student who should be, as the others continued their learning focus.

How can she not look at the chart? It's not because Ms. Smith was a former point guard in basketball and has great peripheral vision. Nope, she isn't even an ex-hoopster. So how was that possible? If you recall, a couple of minutes earlier, she went to the back of the room and glanced at the chart. That's right, she did. And he was the third one on the chart and had what color clip? Purple. It all seems magical, and yet all of it can be taught to every teacher in our schools, districts, and beyond.

Now, why doesn't she look at Marcus? Two reasons. First it gives him attention, which 90 percent of the time was his desire when misbehaving. No reason to reward that. But the other reason is power, which was his desire the other 10 percent of the time. That is why she doesn't look at him. When a teacher pauses and stares at a student, part of their heart too often has flipped to the revenge side. They are mad, hurt, or offended, and they want the student mad, hurt, or offended also. When there is no stare by the adult, the power challenge has most often been avoided. And if you wonder why ineffective teachers cannot use a clip chart (or many other classroom management approaches) effectively, just envision what the most volatile staff member does when they clip a student down. They pause for dramatic effect, stare directly at the student with anger in their expression, and with exaggerated energy clip the student down. And they may sigh loudly while doing it. This is a power grab attempt by the adult. And the power-hungry student isn't going to let them win.

When we try to get revenge on a student wanting power, they will make sure they get revenge on someone, anyone. Maybe not you, maybe not now. But they will get their chance with someone at recess, the lunchroom, the locker-room, or passing time in the halfway.

Sadly, when a teacher makes an incorrect decision or action, they think they are doing it right. This is what they learned. This is what they observed as a student teacher or peer. They did learn from role modeling. It was just the wrong role model. But when a teacher is taught with precision how to do it right so the students behave better, they will try it and typically be rewarded by the results. It has never been the clip charts. It has always been the teacher. But people who are exceptional and those who truly want to get better already knew that. Others want something to blame, and it is always simpler to blame a program.

11

The One Best Way

Sorry to use the title of this chapter as clickbait, but there is no one best way. If there was there would only be one chapter. In reality, no examples involving schools, students, teachers, or people in general are absolute. The examples shared previously are not a guarantee, and naysayers work very hard at squinting to find exceptions. Good for them. However, this is a framework that the best teachers almost always use on a consistent basis. Conversely, most ineffective teachers at best use it on an infrequent or inconsistent basis.

When you were a student, whether it was last year or last century, were you ever in a school where the students knew which teachers were the yellers? In your current school, if you have a staff member like this, can the students in your setting identify the adult who is the yeller? Can the teachers in your school identify the colleagues in the building who are the yellers? In most places, the answers to these questions are all yes. However, the teachers that are most likely to be identified as the yellers may not know that everyone else knows they yell and/or treat students inappropriately. They might not even know it is inappropriate. But they definitely do not want their peers to have a lower regard for them.

Teaching is the most isolated profession though we are never alone. However, at times we can be lonely. Teachers want to be

DOI: 10.4324/9781003492535-14

good. They want to be great. They want to be the teacher the students remember and remember fondly. They want to be the educator that students come back and see, that students miss when they go to the next grade level or a different school. This core is the reason we really can help all teachers become like the best teachers. They want to be the best teachers. Why do you think they chose teaching? They want to make a difference. So, it is safe to assume the vast majority of educators are open to new ideas. We have to help them understand how to apply the approaches the best people take. So they can do the things that are necessary to increase future learning. We want teachers to do the right thing when we are looking, but most of the time they are 'alone' in the classroom and need to have some well-established 'go to's in routine and challenging situations.

Everything Seems Random and Yet Nothing Is

When you observe an outstanding teacher, things seem so easy and so natural. It can appear to an outsider that anyone could do this. And to a slightly jaded insider, it can seem like they get lucky (every year) with the way students behave in their classes. They may seem to have it made, but we know they have worked very hard to become highly effective. They usually seem calm, and seldom hurried, and simultaneously somehow become more accomplished than anyone else. I guess that is why they are the best.

We may think it is chance or luck, but when we examine it closely, we realize it is preparation and practice. Let's teach all teachers how to do assemblies properly. Teach everyone what the best teachers do at assemblies. As we know, it is sitting with their students rather than sitting with peers, standing in the back, or not even going into the assembly. Potentially we have staff members that do not know that or may have forgotten the appropriate thing to do. It isn't just to sit with their students; it is to sit with their most challenging students. We have to help people understand why they need to do this the correct way. The obvious reason we sit next to the most challenging students is so they behave more appropriately. Just using proximity by sitting next to them greatly enhances the chances of proper etiquette. But another reason we need to share this with all staff simultaneously is that if we do not properly supervise our class, we are unprofessionally dumping on a colleague because they now must watch two classes and one of them is ours, and they might not even know the students' names. Effective teachers do the right thing because it benefits the students. Everyone else does the right thing when it benefits them. Effective teachers sit by the students because it helps everyone enjoy the assembly more. Ineffective teachers, once this is shared with the group, are more likely to sit with their students because they do not want their colleagues to think poorly of them.

> Effective teachers do the right thing because it benefits the students. Everyone else does the right thing when it benefits them.

Now, we already know their colleagues think poorly of them because they get dumped on and have to supervise their class as well. However, the ineffective people don't know their colleagues knew they were ineffective. People who are not successful often work very hard to keep their ineffectiveness a secret. Once the secret is out, they likely have more incentive to do what is right by their peers.

The other challenge is typically that the best teachers and the average teachers have similar approaches such as proximity, clip charts, and so on, but the way they implement them can vary widely. When we think back to the clip chart example, by embedding proximity in their teaching on a regular basis, the teacher may walk by the clip chart many times each hour. Thus, the clip chart is not a distraction. However, if a teacher is too stationary and they then head toward the chart, it can become an event. As the teacher heads that way, the students know the only reason for the teacher ever moving in that direction is to clip a student down. The students may even react like it is a game show and be tempted to yell out, "Come on down!" as the teacher darts to the chart. They both use a clip chart. One does it effectively and the other struggles. The best people reflect on what they do. Many less effective people focus on what

> The best people reflect on what they do. Many less effective people focus on what others do.

others do. And in many cases it is the students. Or the parents. Or administration. Things that they cannot directly influence.

This same difference is seen with assemblies. The best teachers and the average teachers sit with the most challenging students. However, this can happen in dramatically different ways. The average teachers might be tempted to sit by the challenging student in revenge mode. They may corner them and lecture pointedly, "You are going to sit by me at this assembly because of your disruptive behavior. And if it doesn't improve, you are going to sit beside me for the rest of the year!" They want revenge and most likely have escalated the lectured student and maybe have even drawn a line in the power sand to prove who is the 'boss.'

So, what is different about the very best teachers? They too sit next to the most-likely-to-converse student. However, they pretend it is all random. It is totally prevention centered. The great teacher is walking their students to the assembly and when they arrive at the facility, they stop and let the students begin to walk in. However, 'coincidentally,' when does the teacher join the group? When the student they need to sit next to happens to be entering the auditorium. The teacher warmly smiles and falls right in line next to the special student. It's all preventative, and yet it seems random. These practices can assist, on a regular basis, everyone in the school. Some of these things should be taught before the school year starts so the tone in the classroom can be appropriately established. Others should be done when they are most needed—prior to open house night, before the first assembly. That is when the desire to learn is most acute. Teaching all staff members how the best people think and behave gives them a chance to think and behave like the best people. And then when they insert these things into their own practices, they actually begin to become more like the most talented and successful peers.

Lunch Supervision

Though this book is focused on how to become like the best classroom teachers, ironically everyone at school (and at home!) can become more effective in any setting if they imitate the practices of the best educators in the school. I learned this when supervising a cafeteria for the first time. One of my early administrative roles was assistant principal in an eighth-grade center. This school had 750 eighth graders. I thought of it as adolescence at its finest.

Anyhow, as the lone assistant principal, one of my roles was supervising the lunchroom. One adult working with 750 eighth graders is not exactly the ideal ratio. However, that was one of my tasks. Figuring out how to do this initially seemed overwhelming. But then I reflected on how the best teachers in the school would do it. So, I decided a starting point would be infusing proximity into my supervision. Thus, every day I made the 'random' rounds in the cafeteria. I always went by the students sitting by themselves and had a short chat. I wanted to make sure that although they were alone, they were not lonely. Then I'd swing by the 'popular kids' table. But I would make it a brief stop because peer dynamics are so essential to adolescents that there was no reason to make other students feel even more inadequate by being overly attentive to the students they may feel inferior to. And I also thought, if I want to congratulate the volleyball team, I do not necessarily need to do so in the lunchroom with the students who got cut from the team being reminded of what they missed out on. Instead, I could swing by practice and stroke their egos all I want without peer jealousy. I'd also try to circulate in varying directions, so I'd have a chance to connect with all 750.

In just a couple of weeks, it seemed like it was going well. It seemed like an organized routine was setting in for myself and the kids. But a problem started to regularly occur. One of the tables was consistently junked up with trash, food waste, and unreturned trays. What to do? Well, I thought, "What would the best teacher in our school do?" Would they try to hunt the kids down? Would they watch the video to identify which students at the table were the biggest problems? Would they call parents, give detentions? Heck, I was an administrator—I could even issue suspensions! Since I was almost wearing a badge of authority, any and all of those options were possible. But what was my real goal? Prevention. I really desired for it never to happen again.

As we mentioned earlier, lunchtimes in schools seldom fall on normal round numbers ending in 5 or 0. Instead, this lunch bell rang at 12:07. So, I had the chance to see how proximity worked with 750 students with independent time. Once I figured out the table, the next day at 12:05 I lollygagged to their location. Surely, I was going to mention, warn, or threaten them about clearing their table, wasn't I? We have got to put a stop to this right now!

If I hadn't reflected on the practices of the best teachers, that may have been my choice. But once I thought about how the most effective educators in the school handle things, it provided an alternative approach. When I walked up smiling, I could not have been friendlier. I just started talking to them about their week, what they were doing this weekend, how the local sports teams were doing, etc. I'd been there two minutes and the 12:07 bell rang. What did I do? Kept talking, asking about the classes, different teachers they had, and so on. I could tell they were getting nervous. Guess what they wanted me to do? Walk away so they could leave their trash and trays on the table. Guess what I did, just kept talking about friendly student-centered things. Finally, they became unsure, so they begrudgingly returned their trays and dumped their trash.

How do we change the one-day climate behavior alteration into an everyday culture? The leader of the group was named Donnie Woodruff. He was a tough, intimidating student. When he walked down the hallway, his peers jumped out of the way. So, since this one day went better, I wrote a handwritten note to Donnie and thanked him for his leadership at lunch. I appreciated him helping with table pickup and said how much I knew the custodians appreciated it as well since they already do so much for the school. I then taped the note to the shelf on his locker to make sure he saw it. Somehow or another we never had trouble with that table again. I'd hear Donnie telling his peers, "Hey loser, take your tray back."

Now, I could have lectured them, punished them, or threatened them. But you know what? Donnie didn't want attention. He wanted power. And if I took or even tried to take his power from him when I was watching, he would have worked to regain it when I wasn't. And let's be honest, there are so many times when we aren't watching.

No Need to Out Quick

One of my part-time jobs was bagging groceries. It was in a large food store in an urban area. The onboarding consisted of this: "Are you Todd?" I nodded. "Lane 6!" That was it.

I went to lane 6 and was going to prove my worth by being the fastest and most efficient bagger in the store. I knew not to put stuff on the bread, keep the cold items together, etc. And I was doing it at breakneck speed. The manager came over and said, "Don't be in a hurry. They are not going to leave without their groceries." Instead, he suggested I chat it up with customers. "Ask how their day is, compliment their shoes, ask their kids what grade they were in, talk about the weather. Make them feel important, special." Rather than leaving in two minutes they departed in four, but the real benefit was that they left feeling better about their experience.

We briefly mentioned this before, but there is no hurry. No need to disrupt everyone to clip down the student who is not behaving correctly. This is doubly true in the classroom. I was not a particularly cooperative student, to put it mildly. I was very smart alec and quick on the draw with comebacks. The very best teachers avoided the fracas. They knew better than to take on my strength. But other, less skilled teachers would always try to win. They regularly wanted to one-up me. However, I practiced every day in every class. I was really good at it. The challenge with taking a student on is that you had better win. Because if you lose today, you lose for the rest of the year. Students like I used to be do it every day because they don't need to have a winning record; they just need you to have one loss.

The Least Important Student

I had to teach my assistant principals that the student who gets sent to the office immediately becomes the least important student in the school. This does not mean we will ever berate or belittle the offender. It just means that we need to remember that if we have 1,500 students in our school and one of them is sent to the office, we still have 1,499 doing the right thing. And our immediate goal is to work to keep it from getting to 1,498. And we do this by making sure we regularly compliment, value, and give attention to the 1,499. Because it is just like in the classroom. If you have one disruptive student, keeping the other 24 on task is essential. Because if you get to 23, then 22, then 21, at some point you do not have a chance anymore.

Now, what about the one student in the office? No principal defends teachers more than I do. No one. I just am not in a hurry. Do you want to know why? I am not in a hurry to deal with the student in the office because there isn't a teacher in the school in a hurry to get them back. And, in many settings, if the administrative assistant that is based in the office is really talented, odds are they can probably deal with that student better than the teacher who sent them to the office.

If you have read any of my books on dealing with difficult people, you'll realize I do not have any interest in only resolving a situation. I have an interest in changing behavior for the long term. That is how the best teachers seem to 'get lucky' every year. Because when the students encounter these outstanding educators, the students behave differently than they do with everyone else. Do you know who is 'lucky' in that classroom? The students who have the good fortune of working with that special teacher.

If we do not reward students (and adults), then they will try to be rewarded by not behaving. This does not mean giving them a tangible reward. In classrooms this means making them feel special, giving them increased confidence, and having them do significant learning—about the subject—and about life. That is the magic of the best.

12

Teach Me How to Filter, Please

The next two chapters are things I have written about previously. I do not like to repeat things but feel that the ideas are essential as we work to help all teachers become like the best teachers. There are certain things that clearly separate the best from the rest, and these are important to share or reshare as needed. In Chapter 3 we explored how the best teachers look at the world; in this chapter we are going to describe how they filter their view to help others see their own world in the best light as well.

Everyone Filters

Everyone has their own view of the world. Some look for the good in others, and others constantly try to sniff out the bad. Some see the glass half full, some see the glass half empty, and others see another dirty dish to wash. We all know people with each of these views but, believe it or not, we may not know which people have each of the viewpoints. The reason is that we don't see how others view the world, but we hear how others filter their view of the world.

There is an Academy Award winning movie that was released in 1997 titled *Life Is Beautiful*. The title may seem misleading because the movie is about a dad and his son who are in a German

DOI: 10.4324/9781003492535-15

concentration camp during World War 2. In order to protect his son from the horrors they are facing, the dad works to make their time a game to guard his son and provide hope. The father saw and knew the reality but shielded his son by filtering what was happening by the way he acted and communicated with his son. Of course, this is a movie and far beyond anything in a school, but it demonstrates how exceptional people use their filter before they communicate with others.

Filtering Is a Choice

When people ask someone how their day is going, the person has a choice in how to respond. Some people consistently say "Great," while others repeatedly say, "Not so well." Both are making a choice on how to respond. This is not right or wrong, but it is true. As a principal I learned the importance of this. If I had a volatile parent in my office named Mr. Jones and I finally got him to calm down and leave in peace, it could be a draining event. Then when I walk out in the hallway and a teacher says, "How is your day going?" I must choose how to respond. I could say, "Oh that Mr. Jones was here, and he is always such an attack dog, and his screaming and cussing was nonstop!" or I could say, "Great, how are you?" If I say the first part and describe the combative Mr. Jones, I might now have teachers in my school who are afraid of any students whose last name is Jones, as well as any students who have stepparents whose name is Jones, etc. Or I could say "Great" and allow that person to carry on in a positive way. Both are options. However, I would respond "Great" simply because it doesn't help the people in my school for me not to. I feel no desire to increase worries or add to others' concerns. This is not a false positive and it is not toxic positivity. I have a very realistic view of this parent, teachers, and our school. I just want to be the filter to keep burdens away from others when possible. Sometimes they have to be shared but many times they do not. We are the filter. It is our choice.

We are the filter. It is our choice.

Teachers continually must decide what to filter and what to share. This is true whether they are communicating with students, families, colleagues, or supervisors. One of the biggest differentiators of the very best teachers is that they excel at filtering. Some average teachers do it as well, but all exceptional teachers do it on a regular basis.

How Many People Know?

If a great teacher has 25 students in their class and they are in a bad mood, how many people in the class know? I will let you ponder that briefly. The buzzer has sounded, and the answer is one, the teacher.

If a negative teacher is in a bad mood, how many people in the school know? You don't need any processing time for this one. The answer is everyone. And everyone doesn't necessarily know because they notice. They know because the negative person announces it. They walk into the classroom and demand, "Don't try me today! I am in a bad mood!" Then they scowl at the students and warn, "I told you I am in a bad mood!" This is a dare for the students to try to take their power.

How Was Your Holiday?

Have you ever worked with anyone whom you were afraid to ask how their summer was when you returned in August for the start of the school year? You were not apprehensive because you knew something unfortunate happened during their break. You were apprehensive because something negative seems to happen every break. And weekend, and holiday … they are exhausting.

You know who they are. Everyone knows who they are. You tentatively inquire, "How was your weekend?" And they blurt back, "Stomach flu, coming out of both ends!" Yikes!

Confession time here: I have never told anyone if I've had the stomach flu. And secretly I consider it a jump start to a diet.

Last year after the winter break, I saw one of those people at a restaurant. I thought I could avoid them, but they caught my eye and the holiday guilt got to me. I was wary but did ask in as friendly and hopeful manner as I could muster, "How was your holiday?" They immediately snapped back, "Southwest Airlines canceled so many flights!" I sympathetically said, "I am so sorry. Where were you stranded?" They said, "Oh, I didn't fly but Southwest Airlines canceled so many flights!"

Whether we want to admit it or not, we all know many people like this. Some are 'friends,' some are neighbors, and some are coworkers. Some unfortunately may be in your family. Hopefully they are out of state.

But in a school, we have students that come from all settings. Some are wonderful, others are heartbreaking, and most are in between. But our responsibility as teachers is to make sure we work with effort and intentionality to keep these things from our classrooms and from our students whenever possible. It is also helpful if we can work at limiting or eliminating the negativity with our peers. Our jobs are difficult on the very best days. Teaching is so draining. It is not just the hours; it is also the intensity. What is an uninterrupted lunch anyhow? Let's work to keep from being a person who dims the lights and increases the woe load. There is no way for a teacher to be truly outstanding if they don't work to help protect and support others in the school. They know the job is a challenge, and they want to add strength not weakness to the setting.

Greeting Students: Everyone Is a Teacher

Have you ever worked with someone who chronically complains? To top that off, have you ever worked with a complainer who regularly threatens to quit? And the real topper, have you ever seen someone who is a terrible, frequent complainer threaten to quit and other people try to talk them out of it!? Unreal.

These people are not just intermittently negative people who sometimes slide whining into conversations. Not at all. They are the worst of the worst. Not only do they regularly complain, but additionally they are not good at their jobs. Why would anyone try to stop them from quitting? I am tempted to start crowdsourcing to donate moving expenses. And I have great faith that families would pitch in and students would chip in their lunch money! You know exactly who I am referring to.

And my very favorite is when the complainers say they are going to quit and go be a greeter at Walmart. My first thought is that they will never hire you. Their standards are higher than that. So, with that in mind, let's reflect for a moment on how the teachers in your school greet the students. We might also touch base on greeting the adults, but that may be treading toward touching the third rail, so let's start with greeting students.

I'd like to begin by suggesting that I hope someone has taught the bus drivers how to greet the students. As we explored in Chapter 3, we do not have control over whether students leave home excited about learning. That is beyond our direct influence. However, teachers have a strong influence regarding how excited students are when they enter their classroom. They have a tremendous impact either way.

But we need to ensure that someone teaches the bus drivers how to greet and work with students. Bus driving is really, really difficult. If we think managing 25 students sitting in front of you is hard—and of course it is—try managing 66 children behind you while you are driving a bus. I don't know how they do it, and I have driven buses with students before. Exhausting!

And, just like the teachers, we need to teach the bus drivers how to manage the students. If we do not teach them, how would they ever learn? A few of them can figure it out on their own, but the numbers are quite small. And if they lose patience while trying to manage their student riders, they will potentially treat them inappropriately. If the bus drivers become frustrated with student behavior, then they will definitely mistreat the students. And if they mistreat the students, the students will in return mistreat them. Then, we may not know how the students left home, but we know for certain how they arrived at school.

We need to make sure the custodians are friendly and professional with students. It is quite easy for students to get revenge on a custodian. Just recall the TikTok videos that circulated a while ago. And it is not a one-way street. We must teach students that they have to be nice to food service. If they wonder why, just remind them that it is very easy for a cook to get revenge on those they are serving.

Now, let's reflect on how the best teachers greet students and how it compares to others. How do average people typically greet students? Well, with many individuals it depends on the date, time of year, and how they are feeling. At the start of the year, they are gung-ho and head butting and high fiving. But when it is a Tuesday in February, they may complain aloud to the class that there are four more days this week and 77 left in the school year. The mood can change with the weather and possibly with which students are present or absent that day.

How do the best educators greet their students—and many times other students they see in the hallway? They are consistently warm and welcoming. It does not depend on the weather, their mood, and the time until the next vacation. Like most things in education and life, the best people have the same goals, just varying paths to arrive there. We have likely seen videos of teachers who have a variety of fancy handshakes, daps, or first bumps, or give knuckles. Each student has their own and somehow the teachers memorize the one they use with each child as they enter the class. This is impressive, but we have no idea of the quality of the teacher. But it looks really cool, and I am jealous of their ability. Additionally, there are teachers who call students by name as they enter class or make eye contact with each child or ask everyone as they enter how their pet is doing. Again, I have no guess as to the effectiveness of each of these individual teachers. However, I am confident that if the teacher does not make it a point to have some level of connection when the students arrive, there is little likelihood they are the best. How we greet the students is a completely personal choice for each teacher. Whether we greet the students consistently and in our own inviting fashion probably has a big determination on the quality of the teacher. If they do it, that doesn't automatically make them exceptional. But if they don't, it removes their hope of being at the highest level. It reminds me of one of my favorite sayings. You do not have to be kind to be a teacher, but you do have to be kind to be a good one.

You do not have to be kind to be a teacher, but you do have to be kind to be a good one.

Early in this book, in Chapter 2, we explored that even with no prior practice we could predict which teachers would be effective teaching remotely during the pandemic. We also felt confident we could identify others who would likely struggle. We found that the ones we thought would struggle teaching virtually might also have the most difficultly teaching in person. Like I said then, it is the same skill set. Consistently being caring does not make you a great teacher, but it sure points you down the correct path.

During the pandemic or anytime we teach virtually, we can greet the students or not. It is up to us. And it doesn't matter the age group; it still means something to people. Outstanding teachers who work with adults in virtual programs still make it a point to make a connection. They do not all look the same. Many look quite different and should. But they all are important, and the outstanding people always work to have a connection. Because they know it matters.

Have you ever worked with someone who doesn't greet the students? Have you ever worked with someone who doesn't greet the adults? Doesn't make eye contact, doesn't even smile, just smile? And if you have ever worked with someone negative who does greet the kids, their tone is something like, "Welcome to the torture chamber!"

I'd like us to reflect on something else. Does it take intelligence to greet students? Nope. Does it take skill to greet students? No (unless somehow you can memorize individual shakes with every student!?). Does it take effort to greet the students? Yes, definitely. You must want to do it and make yourself do it on a regular basis even if you do not want to. You know that you need to and clearly should. That is the core of filtering. You must center on your audience—the students—and what is best for them rather than letting your internal mood set the tone for the class. We all have ups and downs, because we are human. But we can also make sure that we consistently treat our students with regard. Not just because that is our job, but also because that is what students deserve. It is one of the reasons we chose to teach. We want to regularly have a positive impact on others. If we do it one day, it can have a positive impact on the climate in our classroom. If we do it every day, it becomes the culture for the class and an example of how we want everyone to treat others.

When we share things that take effort, not talent, to do, and people choose not to do them, that is probably a bad sign of their commitment to making a positive difference. To have a chance at becoming exceptional, we need people to do two things every day. These two things are to *care* and *try*. If someone cares and tries every day, they always have a chance to continue to improve. When they choose not to do these things—care and try every day— we have probably already seen the cap on their talent potential. Sharing the importance of greeting students and reinforcing the wide variety of ways to do it should be an expectation for every- one in an educational setting. Being the filter limits the negativity in our classroom, which is essential to letting the positivity emerge.

13

The Emotional Modes

There are many things that resonate with some people. You can be drawn to an appealing way of decorating your abode, have a favorite television show, or regularly visit the restaurant you find most appealing.

Teaching also has a variety of things that great teachers pick and choose from to varying degrees—for example, group work, room arrangement, technology usage. These choices do not determine effectiveness and ineffectiveness. Many times the difference maker is not *what* we choose, but how well we do the things we choose. Even what effective teachers choose to filter or not filter from students may vary widely. But treating them with respect and dignity is a constant in order to be the best.

One thing I'd like to share that seems to really resonate with highly effective teachers—and provides a pathway for everyone else to scaffold toward that top tier—is a concept involving emotional modes. I started presenting this a while ago, and it immediately resonated with teachers in a way that was shocking. So many people contacted me afterwards recounting how integrating this into their practices had more impact on student behavior than anything else they had tried. They also added that it has made a

DOI: 10.4324/9781003492535-16

difference in their home life and even in personal relationships. Since then, I shared this in my writings for the first time in the third edition of *What Great Teachers Do Differently* (Routledge, 2020) to make sure people have access to it. The feedback from those who have integrated it in the field compelled me to share it here. It really does seem to be something that highly effective teachers have in common, whether they realize it or not. And equally significantly it is a concept that is easily taught and can be self-monitored. I apologize if you are familiar with this, but maybe thinking how we can help all teachers become the best teachers may allow it to be viewed from a different perspective.

Background

Dr. Eric Berne (1958) explored a concept called Transactional Analysis (TA) that identified three modes or personalities that all people have—adult mode, parent mode, and child mode. Many others have researched and/or tweaked the thinking regarding this idea. Heather Murray (2023) has provided a recent perspective of this work. A few years ago, I attended a workshop where the presenter shared the modes with a renaming frame. They called them business, parent, and child modes and applied them to teaching. Being a principal at the time, I realized how the best classroom managers in my school either knew of this concept or intrinsically infused it into their practice. But very seldom did average classroom managers use this concept in their classes. Or if they did, they were very inconsistent in its use. And the weakest teachers with student behavior seldom if ever used it.

We sometimes hear people say things like, you are either a good teacher or you aren't. That may be true in an immediate snapshot, but it does not have to be true over time. So, we worked as a school to share and apply the three emotional modes and infuse them into what we did in our classrooms and as a school. The results were fascinating. The concept became part of the verbiage in the school. Some teachers even shared it with their students, and they then became better at awareness and self-regulation. These results are why I felt compelled to first share this and to revisit it in this book. I have never seen any one thing help all teachers become more like the best teachers than this concept. Hope it's worth learning for the first time or being reminded of it again.

As leaders we have to teach everyone in our school how to effectively implement the three modes. Bus drivers, custodians, as well as ourselves. It can also permeate the language used in the school among adults. Sharing things like "I used child mode on students on the playground and it became a nightmare." Or helping teachers understand how they can even teach their students how to become self-aware of the mode they are in and self-check if it is appropriate. And, like we mentioned previously, the best time to teach something is when someone needs it. So, this is one of the main concepts that is probably most valuable at the beginning of the year—possibly at the first faculty meeting so that we can help teachers establish the tone they want in each classroom. When people understand the three modes, it helps them implement proximity, clip charts, and redirect appropriately. Without an understanding of this, they may become confused as to why some of these things work for other teachers but not them.

The Three Modes

Everyone has three emotional modes. Research shows that even children, when they turn two or three, have these three modes. They are business, parent, and child mode. The reason this is in a book about educators is that teachers also have three emotional modes—business, parent, child. The reason these modes are so significant is because it turns out that the mode of the teacher determines the mode of the student. Here are the three connections. When the teacher

> **The mode of the teacher determines the mode of the student.**

is in their business mode, the students go into their business mode; when the teacher goes into their parent mode, the students go into their child mode; and when the teacher goes into their child mode, the students go into one of two modes—parent or child. It is very important to remember:

Teacher	Student
Business Mode	Business Mode
Parent Mode	Child Mode
Child Mode	Parent or Child Mode

This is so important to understand because the mode of the teacher is the influence that leads to the mode of the students. It is not the other way around. Or for sure it shouldn't be!

Typically, what mode do teachers want their students in? Business mode. So, to get the students into business mode, the teacher has to first be in business mode. If 95 percent of the time teachers want students in business mode, then 95 percent of the time teachers must be in business mode. We cannot parent mode or child mode anyone into business mode. Think of it as leading, not pushing.

We cannot parent mode or child mode anyone into business mode.

So, what is business mode? It might sound negative and heavy handed, but that is not the meaning. Business mode is kind, polite, and respectful. Maybe it is what businesses should all be, but not all are. If you have a meeting at a high-quality business, here is the tone they should set. "Welcome, we are so glad you are here today. Does anyone need anything before we get started? The agenda is ready, the technology is set up. We are going to have a great day!" They do this with professionalism and personality. They make sure they greet you well. Quite parallel to how the best teachers connect with their students each day.

I learned this my first year as a math teacher and a basketball coach. I think I am funny. No one else in my family agrees, but I really do. After school we would start basketball practice. Simultaneously with working all day teaching math, I would try to think of a new joke. After school, at 3:00, we would start practice, and I would begin with a joke. I don't have dad jokes; I have bad jokes. Anyhow when I would tell a joke, guess what mode I was in? Child is the answer. And after sharing a joke in child mode, guess what mode I put the entire team in? Yep, child mode. My jokes are very short, so as soon as I tell one and hear the groans, I am ready to begin practice so I immediately switch to business mode. To practice as effectively as possible, I want and need my players in business mode. But guess what mode most young people—who are put in child mode by the adult—cannot immediately switch to? Business mode. To recap, I went into child mode, and the team switched into child mode. Then I quickly flipped to business mode but most people and almost all young people do not have the ability to immediately change to business mode.

That is one reason we need to greet the students because making sure they are entering the room in business mode will set the tone for the remainder of the class period. And doing it for each segment of the elementary day and each period in secondary schools is crucial to ensure that the appropriate mode is established.

Earn Their Respect?

We often hear educators say that you have to 'Earn their respect' related to students at the beginning of the year. How are most students the first day of school? What are they like? Nervous maybe. Cautious, reserved? Polite. Friendly. Maybe even respectful. Yep, they are for the most part on that first day respectful. Weird. I thought we had to earn it. But really it is given as a gift at the start of the school year. The students hand it to us on a platter. Now what we do with it is the challenge. Some teachers help that respect nurture and grow all year. And with other teachers, it begins to diminish the second week of school. But few of us had to earn it. It generally is given to all of us.

What mode do we want students to be in the vast majority of the time? Business. What mode do students come to school in on the first day? Generally, it is business. That is part of respect. The students start in business mode, the culture we want to embed into our classroom.

Every teacher has a choice in how they start the year. Some do 'getting to know you' activities. Some do scavenger hunts. And some just start teaching. Which of these you choose does not distinguish the quality of the teacher. How you do them begins the sorting process. Great teachers want students in business mode, so they know to start the year in business mode. You can do 'getting to know you' activities in any mode you want. You can do scavenger hunts in any mode you want. You can start teaching in any mode you want. But, regardless of what activity you choose to begin with, make sure you do it in business mode. Remember the meeting at the local business and how kind, welcoming, and professional they were? That is what we want to establish in every room in our school.

One time I asked an outstanding math teacher how she starts her year. She told me the first thing she does is teach math. I looked puzzled and she shared this: "I have all year to build relationships. I need to make sure that I help every student understand that they can be successful mathematicians. And I help them know that in this class, we call each other ladies and gentlemen, that we always say please and thank you. Only one of us talks at a time so we can respect each other." She said she also shows them how they'll take turns getting their math manipulatives and how they enter and depart class each day.

This was an urban setting, and she was the best classroom manager and the most popular teacher in the school. She 'earned' their respect by teaching them to be respectful in business mode.

One February 14 I happened to be in a third-grade classroom and observed a teacher doing their Valentine's Day party in business mode. I can still hear her tone and picture her mannerisms. She was calm and just had a happy expression that seemed embedded on her face. In such a soft tone she said, "As you know, today is a special day that we have been looking forward to. It is February 14—Valentine's Day, named after Saint Valentine. We have each been making special Valentine boxes which are lined up against the wall in alphabetical order. Don't they all look wonderful!? Each of us has brought 24 Valentines today to give one to each of our special friends so that no one is left out. We will go two at a time and place the special Valentines in ..."

It is soothing just remembering how the best teachers do everything. Special things seem special. Routine things seem special. And they make every student feel special. Amazing. Business mode. The culture of the best teachers.

In Chapter 11 we explored assemblies and how teachers can differ in how they approach them. We realized many teachers sit with their students, and often the better ones sit with the most challenging students. However, they do so in differing ways. Some do it by threatening/lecturing the student, "You are going to sit by me at this assembly and at every assembly the rest of the year!" The revenge mindset demonstrated here is either parent or child mode (it is scary that sometimes we cannot tell the difference). Thus, even though they were likely in child mode before the abrupt lecture, for sure they are now riveted in child mode. And, sadly, if the verbal outburst by the teacher is witnessed by other students, they now are pulled into child mode as well.

What about the other teacher who 'randomly' turns when the student walks by on the way to the assembly? The teacher warmly smiles and is excited they get to sit next to the student. Prevention. Whatever mode the student is in is irrelevant to the teacher using business mode. And not only does this assist the challenging student to meld into business mode, but any students who witnessed the exchange are likely to transition to or remain in business mode as well.

> **Whatever mode the student is in is irrelevant to the teacher using business mode.**

The Challenging Student

Let's return to the first day of school. A teacher has 25 students in class. 24 of them came to school respectful. And the other one was the disruptor. That's not good. So, on that first day the 24 respectful students started the year in business mode. The other one was in child mode. Well sadly, I was usually the one in child mode as a student. Wanting attention. Always the cut up. And my number one goal, starting on the first day, was to get the other students in child mode. People/students like me want everyone else in child mode. Do you know why? Because people think I am funnier when they are in child mode. I get more attention when my peers are in child mode. It is easier for me to impress the pretty girl or the cool guy when I am in child mode if they are also in child mode. But even though I have a very strong personality, I cannot get the other students in child mode by myself. I need one other person's assistance. Do you know which other person I need in order to transition the other students into child mode? The *teacher*. That's it. That is the key to the magic kingdom. That is why students like me are always trying to annoy the teacher.

See, I cannot get my peers in child mode by myself. I need your magic power because you are the teacher. My goal is to get you mad at me. My aim is to get you to inappropriately go into parent or child mode toward me. Cause when you lose your temper, when the teacher overreacts, they are always in either parent or child mode. It doesn't change me; I was already in child mode. So, what is affected? The mode of the other students. When you yell at me, are sarcastic toward me, or even throw darts at me with your glaring eyes, the conversion has started. What conversion? The other students have started to make the switch to child mode because you went incorrectly into either parent or child mode. One at a time or all at once, it doesn't matter to me. I just need them to join the child mode team. And once you provide assistance and the pretty girl or the cool guy laughs at me, I will be very unlikely to enter or stay in business mode while in your class. That is all the reward I needed. Thank you.

Now you know how we lose the 24 students by getting them out of business mode. But what about the challenging student? Is there any hope of transitioning them into business mode? Yes, there is. But like most things that really make a difference, it is simple; it's just not always easy. The key? Keep the other 24 in business mode. That is it. Do you know why that works? Because in your class—not recess, passing time, or in the hallway—in your class if the cool guy and the pretty girl are consistently in business mode, guess what mode I must go into to impress them? Business mode. That is how it works and that is how life works. From age 3 to 103, we want to make a positive impression; we want to have people like us. If it works best in business mode, we switch. If it is easier to make people like us in child mode, we switch then as well. That is the key to classroom management. Get all students in business mode. If you have that, you have your students. Keep the

24 and you have a great chance of adding the other lone holdout. The outcast wants to be an insider. They can get others to join their club, or the others can recruit them. But the adult in the room is the compass.

Clean Your Bedroom!

Is it possible to get children to clean their bedrooms or is that just a fantasy? You may feel that in your house, it is just a dream. Well, let's see if we can come up with a possible solution.

Let's say you have three daughters, and you cannot get the middle one—Alexa—to clean her room. You would like her to clean her room in what mode? Business of course. But you are frustrated because she is in what mode? Child. Because it seems like a Battle Royal and because you are tired of asking/telling her, you go into what mode? Parent or child. So, you reach your limit and curtly say, "I've told you a dozen times to clean your room." You were in parent or child mode, and Alexa was already in child mode. No loss, right? Well, she is actually adding recruits. Not only is she even more dug into child mode, but her sisters who were not even involved overhear this, and guess what? They weren't even invested in the situation but now they have chosen teams. The youngest sister goes into child mode, and you know what that means. She mocks you behind your back and mocks Alexa to her face. Your oldest daughter goes into parent mode because you were in child mode. Do you know what parent mode is for her? 'Mother Hen.' So, she says, "Don't worry Alexa, I'll help you clean your room." This makes you even madder and you tell her, "No you won't!" Let the games begin.

The risk of inappropriately leaving business mode with one child is the impact it can have on the others. Just like in the classroom. You cannot parent mode anyone into business mode. You have to business mode them.

Sharing examples from home can touch the emotions of staff members and help them realize how these approaches can be escalating or even hurtful. When we personalize them to situations outside of the school, they can also be regularly practiced and reinforced within ourselves.

It Is Not an Event; It Is a Drumbeat

The challenge with business mode is consistency. We need to start the day in business mode and work to maintain that tone. Please remember it is kind and friendly. Effective teachers tell jokes in business mode. They know that students, especially the most challenging ones, need to feel and understand what business mode is. And when students inappropriately go into child mode, the only way they can recover is if the adult in the room pulls them back by having a business mode culture in the classroom.

Follow any middle or high school student with multiple classes around for a day. Any student—male, female, high achiever, struggling academically, any. Watch how they switch modes as they enter the room. The regular mode of the teacher determines the regular mode of the students. Believe it or not, the biggest determinant of student mode is teacher mode. We may feel that it is the peers in the room, but they do not have the greatest impact. It is the teacher. Here are some examples.

It Is the Teacher

Have you ever been in a school where you could predict which teacher was going to send the most students to the office this year ... and every year? Is it because of the students in the room? Is it based on the quantity of kids who have received participation trophies? Of course not; we all know the biggest determinant is the teacher. Every year.

Well, what does that have to do with modes? As you follow students around at the secondary level and they quickly change modes as they walk into each of their classrooms, your instinct may be to assume that is because of the classmates in that period. Well, I want you to think of one specific example. A challenging student walks into the single best teacher in the school's room.

The very best. What mode does the student switch to? In the other five hours of the day they go to child mode, but in this class—and only this class with the best teacher in the school—they go into business mode every day. But something is different today. The student notices as soon as they walk in. The outstanding teacher is not here today and in their place is a last-minute, ineffective substitute. The challenging students can literally smell the fear and low self-confidence of the weak substitute. So, what happens is the disruptive student immediately goes into their best 'look at me' routine. They have been waiting all year to let it out in this class, and this is their chance. Child mode baby, and we are all going to join the funfest. And when they do, students who never act up can't pass up the opportunity, and it is total chaos. Child mode on steroids. Class is destroyed.

The next day the disruptor flies into the room, sees that the best teacher is back, and business mode it is. It's always the adult. Some of the adults pretend it isn't and maybe even wish it isn't, but we all know it is.

Arguing

In any relationship with two people—husband–wife, two partners, boyfriend–girlfriend, teacher–student—in any relationship, if two people are together and either one of them is in business mode, they will seldom, if ever, argue. Anyone, either one. And if there are two of us and we would like to argue less, we need one of us to be in business mode. For one of us, to be in business mode is a goal. We might be hoping for the other one to join us in business mode. But wanting to make the partner be the initial transitionary to business mode is probably a wish. However, if we meet our goal, we will usually get our wish. If we can enter and maintain business mode, the dynamic will most likely make a positive switch. Change now, affect the climate. Never change back, impact the culture. In the classroom and in relationships.

Even if we need to send a student to the office, we can choose which mode to do so in. If we do so in child/parent mode, we might stare at the student and loudly holler, "You need to go to the office!" They get the attention they may have desired, and we may have drawn a line to initiate a power struggle. Even after the student departs, the rest of the students are now in child mode.

However, if we think back to the chapter on proximity, when the timing is right, we sidle up to the student and whisper, "Kevin, you need to go to the office." This student was limited in their reward for attention, and there is no public battle line drawn. And maybe more importantly, the other 24 students remain in business mode.

Consistency

One of the most challenging things for everyone in life is consistency. Exercising one day is doable; exercising every day is much more of a challenge. However, we must work to be in business mode if we expect students to be in business mode. They deserve it, but so do you.

Think of a typical situation where a teacher sends a student to the office. What mode was the student in? Child. What mode did the teacher want the student in? Business. And most likely what mode was the teacher in? Parent. This will never work.

We need to continually work to be in business mode and expect the same from the students. It is not easy, but it is essential to being our best. If we work to stay in business mode, it will help make great strides to having the kind of consistent learning environment that the best teachers establish and maintain in the classrooms. We must focus ourselves and remind others in our setting about being in business mode. At work, at home, and in life. The students deserve it, your family deserves it, and so do you.

Part IV

Timeless Truths and New Learnings

14

The Learning Relationship

We often hear that in schools we need to first establish relationships. I am not here to debate as much as to define. Define what we mean by relationships. It would be wonderful to have deep, lasting relationships with every student. There is clearly no downside. But if a teacher has 150 students a day or is a specialist at the elementary level, they may have twice that or more. That doesn't mean they cannot have significant relationships with students. But one way to think about it is that they can build learning relationships with every student. That is what the best teachers do better than everyone else. It separates them from most of their peers. This is not to diminish personal connections, but it expands it to an equally significant and impactful connection.

Traditionally we might think that relationships are grounded in asking a student about their puppy. Absolutely nothing wrong with that. But if that is our only connection, at some point the puppy becomes a dog and it may even get tiring to the student. This is not a criticism at all. Far from it. What we are working to develop is an understanding that lasting relationships with students at some point almost always become grounded in or at least connected to learning. This is a school year, not a dinner party. Thus, we must establish depth at some point, or we really do not connect. If a person has a first date and the suitor is very outgoing

DOI: 10.4324/9781003492535-18

and friendly, this is a great start. But before long we may need something deeper and more significant to keep the connection moving forward. And in the classroom, it is a learning relationship. This has been mentioned previously, but hopefully this chapter will expand and reinforce how essential this relationship is and how it supplements interpersonal relationships with our students.

Understanding Connections

The problem with thinking the first-date excitement will last is that you have already seen them in their best outfit. They have shared their funniest jokes and stories. And before long, you know their favorite movies and bands. To deepen the connection, we have to move to more significant things. Our dreams, hopes, loves, and vision of the future. The richness makes the connection last. This is what the best educators we know are able to do. And the best musicians. And even the best actors and entertainers.

The Poor Lecturer

When we hear someone is a poor lecturer, we often immediately understand and can name more than a few poor lecturers ourselves and recall how tedious it was to be in their class. A common refrain to improve the poor lecturer is we need to reduce the amount of lecture. This is a comment that is always repeated. The problem is lecture. We need to reduce the amount of lecture. This is portrayed as the issue with poor lecturers—they use the direct instruction approach too frequently. This way of thinking is why it is so difficult to solve problems. We hear from many vantage points that to reduce 'poor lecturing,' we need to minimize the percentage of lecture in that classroom. Sadly, this common way of thinking is most likely incorrect, and that is why poor lecturing is a timeless issue. It is because we think the lecture is the issue. Nope. It is that this lecture is poor. We need to eliminate 'poor,' not eliminate lecture.

In many settings, the best teachers use lecture some of the time. Some outstanding educators may use it quite often. And do you know why it works? Because they are really good at it. They have already gotten rid of the 'poor' but haven't eliminated the lecture. It is almost always more common to attempt to change the program or practice than it is to improve the people. That is why most attempts to improve schools fall away. They are focused on the wrong thing—the program—rather than the variable that matters most—the people.

One of the things that separates the best from others is that they have an accurate sense of self. They are correctly aware of how they come across and how they are being received by others. As we have shared before, outstanding people often arrive at similar outcomes though they take varying paths. Great lecturers and outstanding educators know how they are viewed by others. They know if the learning is connecting with the students.

Some do it by simply reading body language. Others do it by asking students to give them a thumbs up or thumbs down if they understand. And others selectively call on two students because they know if those two students got it, it probably made sense to their typically more successful classmates. Conversely, less effective lecturers—and paralleling that, educators who are not as high quality—struggle with this. They are not aware of how they are received. They may think they know, but they are wrong.

If you go into a poor lecturer's classroom, how long does it take you to notice the students are completely disengaged? Five minutes, 15 tops. If you had to be in there for a full hour, you might feel the desire to stick a letter opener in your thigh just to make sure you are still alive. Now there is a chance that poor lecturer may have asked students about their puppy or their favorite TV show. But, like the first date, that connection dissipated quickly.

The Large Lecture in a College Auditorium

Did you attend or know anyone who attended a large university? If you did, recall or ask them to recall if they ever had a class with 100 or more students in a large lecture format. Now, did you ever happen to have at least one professor who, even in this setting, was really good? Really, really good? Many of us did. And we had many that were not good. It was not the format, the lecture. It was the quality and ability of the person delivering the content.

What is quite important to recall is how you felt about that professor. You respected them, you valued them, and they may even be at the top of your list from college. If you had a collegiate experience like this, you did feel like you had a relationship with the instructor, even if they never knew your name. It is called a learning relationship.

There is a similar effect at times with concerts and celebrities. If anyone you know—including you—has a singer, band, or musician that they love when they see them in concert, even in an arena of 10,000 fans, somehow they are able to make that connection. Do you know any Swifties that almost feel like Taylor Swift is their bestie? It is because, somehow, she makes a personal connection with people she doesn't know personally.

If you see a celebrity that you really admire, there may be nervousness or excitement. You meet them and start telling them they were in your favorite movie or in the show you have streamed five times. They made you feel connected through their work. This is similar to a learning connection in a school. They may not be the same, but there is some parallel in the feelings and emotions that are involved. Because of their talent, skill, and appeal, you feel emotionally attached, and they did not even know you had a puppy.

Outstanding teachers do this in a comparable way. They just receive less pay to do it. But when they do it is not based on how good their next movie is or if you end up liking the song they just dropped. It is because they have made a permanent difference in how you think and learn.

Reducing Poor Lecture

So, how do we reduce ineffective lecture? Teach the teachers a better way. Don't just mandate that they reduce the percentage of time they lecture. Poor lecturers lecture because it is the best approach they have. It is like classroom management:

The best way to reduce or eliminate practices that are less than stellar is to introduce, teach, explain, and reinforce better approaches. When someone implements a new methodology in their class-

The best way to reduce or eliminate practices that are less than stellar is to introduce, teach, explain, and reinforce better approaches.

room and it works, they will readily drop the less effective one. The don't do it because they were 'made to.' They do it because they have a more successful practice.

Relationships and Learning

Please do not take any of this chapter as a dig at relationships. Instead, focus on the types of relationships that must be in place to be a highly effective teacher. Pretend you have a child, and you get to choose their teacher next year. But you only get to choose the teacher based on a description. Would you choose the teacher who has highly engaging lessons every day, or would you choose a teacher who attends your child's basketball game once a month? Well, I don't know what you would choose. But in practice, families would want their child to have the teacher who consistently has engaging lessons. No doubt. And, think of this, if they are not instructionally engaging in the classroom, the student may not even want them at their game, or it would definitely be less impactful having them there. And, to a parent, if you can ensure your child has a teacher that regularly has highly engaging lessons, you would take them whether they even attend an outside activity or not.

This does not mean that it isn't important to be involved outside the classroom when you can. It just means that you want to have your students be highly involved *in* your classroom. Then they will celebrate and remember you every day. Including when you come to their game.

15

The Eyes (and Ears) Have It

Teaching people is a wonderful way to learn. And the better the teaching, the higher the learning. If we can integrate observations, role plays, and demonstrations into the learning it can be a rich and powerful experience. Rather than go into detail about these ideas—entire books have been written by people much smarter than me on many of them—the purpose is to provide exposure to ideas and concepts. They will need to involve people in your school, and some will need to be provided to your teachers at specific times of the year. Hopefully these learning experiences are beneficial and some of them are powerful supplements to the practices of those in your school. They are designed specifically to help all your teachers become like your best teachers.

The Mutual Exchange

The idea behind the mutual exchange is to have teachers go into each other's classrooms in nonjudgmental, nonevaluative ways. They can be specific in their aim, but they can also be a general starting point for teachers in your school to feel comfortable with observing, sharing, and learning from each other.

One of the best ways to begin this is to start with your new teachers and your best teachers. The reason you might want to

DOI: 10.4324/9781003492535-19

have it be an exchange, especially when you first initiate it, is to make the pairings seem like they're peer to peer, versus sending someone in to learn from a master teacher. One benefit of pairing your new teachers and your best teachers can be the possible development of a subculture. Another reason, especially if this is the starting point for your school, is that the first time this is done has a high likelihood of having a positive result. The new teacher is likely to gain a great deal from the best teacher—especially if you hired well—and the best teacher is likely to reinforce the new teacher by complimenting their practices.

Pineapple Charts

Pineapple charts are simply a visual display somewhere in the school that all teachers regularly see and can access that allows teachers to share things they are doing that day that might be of value for others to come and observe. It communicates a welcoming tone and helps others focus in on specific things of interest. Jennifer Gonzalez (2016) very effectively introduced this concept to the masses, so its popularity has become widespread.

Ghost Walks

Though these sound like scary haunted house tours, ghost walks are when teachers visit other classrooms when students are not present. They can then share the decisions they made and the rationale behind choices of desk/table/furniture placement, bulletin boards or other visuals, resource materials they use, etc. These can be beneficial to all but may be particularly valuable as new teachers are setting up their initial classes.

Individual or Group Walk Throughs

These can also be called learning walks or a variety of other names. The purpose is to allow individual teachers or groups to observe practices in classrooms. They can be general observations or timed to fit a specific focus or lesson. Sometimes leadership is involved as part of the group and other times it is totally teacher driven.

Some Observation Supports

Principals or instructional coaches can be of value to facilitate substitutes or teaching assistants to cover classes to free up teachers to visit. They can also provide class coverage themselves, as well as logistical support.

Leaders may also want to design or support the follow-up as necessary. Some people can observe on their own and apply it to personal practices and others may need more guidance.

Classroom Management Visits

With newer teachers there can often be a desire to observe highly successful classroom managers in action. This is a wonderful idea and practice. One caution is that if a person wants to observe a great classroom manager, it may be important to visit their class early in the year so they can hear some of the language and tone the outstanding teacher uses to establish and share clear expectations. The other reason that the timing might be more beneficial early is that after a while in a great teacher's classroom, their management approaches can become so embedded in the teaching, it is more difficult to even realize they are impacting student behavior. With things like proximity and redirection in an outstanding teacher's class, it may not be as easy to see and understand how purposeful and intentional they are in the best teachers' classes.

This is a generalization, but it might be of value when thinking through the timing:

In a great teacher's classroom, an observer might need to visit the classroom early in the year to see classroom management.

In an average teacher's classroom, an observer can go in any day of the year to see classroom management as it never really becomes embedded.

In an ineffective teacher's classroom, an observer may be able to stand in the hallway and hear their classroom management.

Calling Parents

Calling parents can be a scary thing for new and veteran staff members alike. We could set up mock calls, which is of value. Also, a principal could invite teachers in to watch and listen to them call parents—particularly challenging parents. They would get to hear specific wording and see how the principal protects the school and supports the staff when interacting with family members. *Dealing with Difficult Parents* (Routledge, 2016) and *A School Leader's Guide to Dealing with Difficult Parents* (Routledge, 2016) may provide some specificity for you and everyone in your school. Rather than the principal telling new teachers they will support them, the teachers themselves have the opportunity to see, hear, and feel it themselves.

Back-to-School/Open House Night

One of the first events new teachers might participate in is open house or back-to-school night. Sometimes it is called 'meet the teacher.' If a couple of outstanding teachers could demonstrate what they say, where they stand/sit, and how they communicate with parents, it could make a potentially nerve-wracking experience a little more settling for new staff members.

Parent Teacher Conferences

If highly effective teachers could demonstrate or role play how they approach parent teacher conferences shortly before they occur, it could be a powerful learning experience for new, and all, staff members. Seeing and hearing how they are handled adroitly by skilled colleagues can allow these possibly stressful events to be more comfortable.

Recordings

Having technology and organizational support can allow all teachers to self-record for personal reflection. The recordings can also be shared with respected colleagues so they can provide suggestions for a particular class, student, or lesson. Rather than having you just explain how you did something, they would have the chance to see your actions and provide guidance.

Recordings can also be done to replace walk throughs and visits so that all staff can learn from them. Additionally, with the tremendous shortage of substitutes and personnel at many schools, this may be a way to learn if we cannot directly visit a class.

There is no one best way to help new staff and all staff grow. However, in most schools we have people that are experts at specific aspects of teaching. We have others that are great with parent communication when calling or conferencing. The opportunities are rich in all schools. When we get to observe and learn from each other, it allows the knowledge of one to

When we get to observe and learn from each other, it allows the knowledge of one to become the knowledge of all.

become the knowledge of all. No one steals a worse idea, and these connections are essential in helping everyone become like the very best.

16

Understanding High Achievers

To help all teachers become like the best teachers, we have to ensure that the best teachers are supported, reinforced, and valued on a regular basis. Otherwise, they may lose some of their spark and effectiveness. Using them as a role model and not causing them to lose their credibility with their peers is a very delicate dance. But remember as a leader that outstanding educators can make great boogie partners. But only if handled correctly.

The Perfection Comparison

One of the most critical components to understand about your very best people is how much pressure they place on themselves. That is one of the reasons that they are so incredibly effective, and that is one of the reasons the leader must work effectively with them. High achievers compare themselves to perfection. Low achievers compare everyone else to perfection. High achievers often find fault in themselves. Low achievers regularly find fault in others.

DOI: 10.4324/9781003492535-20

Driven by Confidence?

Though it may seem that high achievers are driven by confidence because of how flawlessly they perform and how seldom they seem rattled, in many cases high achievers are actually plagued by insecurities. How can that be? Well, if you compare yourself to perfection, how often do you reach that level? Basically never. So, to continue to grow, often the best and brightest may work more to avoid failure than to reach success. Many high-achieving athletic coaches disclose that they dread losing more than they enjoy winning.

This may cause a twinge of concern, but hopefully it also sprinkles in plenty of self-reflection from leaders as to the best way to support the very best. A half attempt at humor here, but ineffective teachers seem to have so much confidence that they can go ahead and teach when none of the students are paying attention. We can picture educators that fit that description. Maybe it is obliviousness more than it is confidence. However, in a nonhumorous description which students do the best teachers need to have the proper focus before they 'go ahead and teach'? The obvious answer is all of them. The best teachers feel they are responsible when students do not succeed. The best teachers have an internal focus for success. They feel like it is their responsibility to provide the guidance and direction appropriate for every and all students in their class. An internal locus of control.

For many less effective teachers, it seems that they have an external focus for success—or blame—it just depends how you are looking at it. With a teacher with lower results, on a regular basis often they blame the students, the families, administration, and so forth. The challenge with this external locus of control is there is no reason to try to improve because you see it as something someone else must change first. And this can be very reinforcing to low achievers, but it keeps them riveted in the lower band. So as a leader we must be highly aware of how things impact our best.

We Are Off to a Great Start! Let's Keep It Up!

Many schools have a high-energy start to the year and the leaders want to reinforce that momentum. The same thing is true in many classes. We get off to a good start and we want to keep it going. One of the most common things we hear leaders say in these circumstances is, "We are off to a great start, let's keep it up!" That almost rolls off our tongues because we have heard others say it on many occasions. But if we look through the lens of the best, we can see how it may actually have a negative impact on our most important members. When we say, "We are off to a great start, let's keep it up!" which half of that do the most effective people focus on? "Keep it up!" Do we need to remind your very best teachers to keep up the effort? No, that has been a constant voice in their head every day since they were little. They continually remind themselves to do their best, not slack off, and so on. When they hear a leader say it, the result is not a closer relationship with the leader. Instead, it causes them to put a distance between themselves and the leader, as the leader has added pressure on someone who is already at their limit because of self-assigned pressure.

Ironically, the best people focus on 'keep it up,' but the people we really are trying to motivate center on which part? "We are off to a great start." This seems like a nice thing, and the attempt is that for sure. But rather than the additional burden of 'keep it up,' the same thing can be accomplished with the shorter, "We are off to a great start! Thank you all so much." Each situation is different, but high achievers are often so focused on what they haven't done that we need to be cautious not to add to their self-inflicted pressure load.

This Has Been Great So Far

I do a lot of presenting around the world. Sometimes I will do a full-day session. (Any of you who have heard me might feel that an hour with me feels like a full day!) Recently I was presenting all day, and when we broke for lunch one of the audience members raced up to meet me and very enthusiastically said, "This has been great so far!" They meant this from their head to their toes. They meant it from their heart and their soul.

I thanked them and walked away with a funny feeling. I realized that to a high achiever, that is not a compliment. It is actually a burden. When someone tries to reinforce another person and they have a qualifier like "so far," the high achiever feels more pressure because the complimenter has left themselves an emotional opening to withdraw their praise if the remainder of the day does not meet their self-imposed standard. Saying, "This has been great!" accomplishes the same thing with a high achiever without the additional baggage of 'so far.' And the person who said it consciously or unconsciously is reserving the right to change their mind. Nothing wrong with having that right—we all do, but it lessens the power of influence when we verbally say it. Especially with the most driven people.

Evaluating High Achievers

Many evaluation systems are seen as less than ideal. Many evaluators may also struggle with finding the time and energy to effectively apply the evaluation process correctly. One of the limitations is understanding how the forms and process impact the best teachers in a school. A common format when there is an observation—brief walk through or a 30 to 50-minute stretch—is to then follow up with a form that is used each time these visits occur. A way too common part of the systems is that the forms on each observation require something like 3 plusses and 1 minus. Meaning that each visit the feedback is supposed to include three praises and an area of growth and/or improvement. The potential damage from this is feeling the need to regularly suggest improvements for your best and brightest. Understand that they are always looking to get better; that is an inherent part of their make-up. They are regularly reflecting on how a lesson or interaction went. The tone with which they spoke to a student. Or why several members of the class did poorly on an assignment. Many high achievers on a regular basis place a burden on themselves that is closer to this ratio—2 plusses and 16 minuses. As a leader, the best thing we can do for the vast majority of our staff members, and especially the best staff members, is to look to regularly reinforce the positives and allow as many minuses as possible to stem from self-reflection rather than a judgmental viewpoint.

And as leaders, if we feel obligated to give formal feedback every time we walk through a classroom, that can be exhausting and an actual disincentive to go in classrooms as often as we'd like and as frequently as we should.

Hire Good People and Get Out of Their Way

One of the most popular leadership/management sayings we continually hear people say is that the key to a successful organization is to "Hire good people and get out of their way." This is used by people in business, organizations, and schools. And it sounds so catchy. And, like many things that are repeated by average or ineffective people, it is also wrong.

Good people do not want leaders to get out of the way. The only exception to this is if the

> **Good people do not want leaders to get out of the way.**

leader is not effective and actually makes the job of the employees more difficult to be successful. Instead, employees want leaders to hire good people and:

Show the way
Lead the way
Protect the way
Point the way
Reinforce the way
Protect them from others who block their way
Deal with people who don't know the way
Improve or remove people who are in the way
Make sure that ineffective coworkers are out of the way

These are just a few of the things that people in an organization want from leadership. And the better the people are, the more they want, expect, and need these things from those who are in the top positions of the organization. When an angry parent shows up unexpectedly to berate a teacher, they do not want the leader to get out of the way. When there is a bully coworker, the others in the school do not want the leader to get out of the way. When a new employee is just starting, they do not want the leader to get out of the way.

The only people that want the leader out of the way are employees with poor leaders and poor employees with good leaders. Otherwise, they want leaders in the trenches providing guidance, support, and direction. And the high achievers are the first to desire and support effective leaders. Because in addition to all their other gifts, they are often the ultimate team player who wants the organization to be a true success.

Blanket Monkeys

One of my books is titled *Shifting the Monkey* (Solution Tree, 2014). It was written for businesses and was in airport bookstores and adopted by companies worldwide. One idea from it I'd like to share is called the 'Blanket Monkey.' The main idea of a blanket monkey is that instead of dealing with the one person doing something wrong, the leader incorrectly throws a monkey on everyone. Have you ever been to a faculty meeting where the principal was talking to all the teachers about one teacher? Browbeating the entire staff with a diatribe such as this?

> "Sometimes some of you teachers are coming late to school. Sometimes, some of you."

Everyone knows the principal is talking about one person but is inappropriately throwing a guilt monkey on everyone. The reason I am sharing this example in the chapter on leading high achievers is that they are the ones who are most offended when the leader blanket monkeys the entire staff. When the principal says, "Sometimes some of you teachers are coming late ..." guess which teachers are most offended? The good ones. Do you know what they are thinking? "What are you talking to me for, why aren't you talking to her?" And they look for the teacher the principal is referring to at everyone's expense and the teacher notices, "They are not even here yet!"

Have you ever been in a school where a note comes around to all faculty that says: "Some of you have not turned in your grades yet!"

Which teacher is most concerned when they receive that broad, sweeping note? The good ones! The ones whose lives are already completely driven by guilt. The best teachers run down to the office and ask the records clerk, "Have I not turned in my grades yet?" So, the best people are offended, and we have wasted the time and energy of our top staff members and the records clerk because we took the fearful way out and delivered a blanket monkey on everyone instead of having an individual conversation with the constant slacker. And what even adds to the nonsense of using this approach is that when we address the entire group over the misbehavior of one or two, the actual result is that we let the slackers off the hook. Do you know what they are thinking when they get the whole group correspondence? "Oh good, there must be a whole bunch of us, that's why they sent the note."

Leaders cannot risk diminishing their credibility with the best people because they are afraid of or unsure how to deal with the loafers or malingerers in the school. The best people know it is wrong, so it is essential that we learn to do it right.

> **Leaders cannot risk diminishing their credibility with the best people because they are afraid of or unsure how to deal with the loafers or malingerers in the school.**

The Leader's Pet

One of the definitions of a superstar teacher is that they must be respected by their peers (Whitaker, 2020a). Without this respect, they will not be able to have the informal influence needed to help move their colleagues and the school in a positive direction. One thing that damages this perception is if the best teachers are viewed as the principal's pet. Now, they can, and probably should be the principal's pet. But they cannot be seen in that light. Because if they are seen as the favorite, they may forfeit the informal peer pull that they have.

So, since we value their opinions, how can we touch base with them regularly without crossing the line? Well, effective leaders have many ways of doing this. One, you could ask everyone their opinion, so they are all included. And with many high achievers, they may be at the school early or stay late, so you may take advantage of that window when there are no peers seeing the interactions.

Believe me, the truly exceptional teachers do not want to be seen as the leader's pet. You have teachers who want to be seen that way, but those teachers are not the best.

The Informal Seating Chart

Another way to help the best teachers avoid being seen as the principal's favorite involves the seating arrangement in meetings. When possible, do not sit next to these teacher leaders. Whoever you station yourself closest to has their power diminished. So, when you are next to the best, their informal influence is automatically reduced. Instead, sit next to the least effective and/or most disruptive staff member. You lessen their comfort and increase the comfort of the highflyers. Isn't this exactly what great teachers do? They randomly sit next to the students who might be the weakest in self-control. That is exactly what the best leaders do as well. It is not a power play so be kind, friendly, and warm as you sit next to them. It empowers the best and weakens the rest. Remember to be kind to everyone as you do this. Recall that in a great teacher's classroom, every student feels like they are the favorite. And, as we all know, they are not.

Balancing the Burden

We have shared many things that seemingly add to the burden of your high achievers. Naturally, in some instances, they do take on an increased workload. If so, then we need to have other instances where the opposite occurs. Do not punish the best people for being good. Make sure you do not ask them to or let them serve on too many committees or take on an overabundance of roles. As you delegate tasks and responsibilities, make sure you include everyone. And delegate the importance of the task to the talents of the person. Don't ask your best people to host the holiday party and lead the math curriculum. Think which of these tasks is most important to the growth of the school and have them do that, but share the wealth with everyone.

Do not ask your most talented secretary to fold and staple. If they are folding and stapling, they cannot focus on the most significant areas that their talents can impact. And, if we do not ask less-eager workers to do more redundant tasks, like fold and staple, potentially they are able to dodge having much of an equitable workload with others in the school. And as a leader, people are not nearly as mad at the avoiders as they are upset with the enablers who allow the avoiders to dodge equal or even minimal responsibilities. By the way, that is you, the leader.

If you have three new teachers and we have the three best teachers serve as mentors, it may seem unfair. But we need to start this process with them. If we choose the mentors correctly, we potentially have six outstanding teachers to serve as mentors the following year, 12 after that, etc. There are things we absolutely need our best teachers to do. Just make sure they are the most important things, as these individuals are so essential to our school.

The Gifts of the Best

There are many contributions the best employees give to our school. Here are a few:

> The best teachers want everyone to succeed; they see the world as an unlimited sum game.
>
> The best teachers want the principal to succeed; they know if the principal is not effective, it will limit the growth of the school.
>
> The best teachers may be the only ones who will look you in the eye, tell you the truth, and not be part of the rumor mill. They are very trustworthy.
>
> The best teachers have a whole organization-wide vision. They go far beyond what is best for them and instead desire what is best for 'us' or what is best for 'the school or the district.'

The best teachers have an internal impetus for change. They want to change when it will improve the school or lead to better outcomes for the students.

These are some of the gifts that the best teachers provide to the school, the building leaders, their colleagues, and their students. We must make sure we regularly treat them as a gift because that is what they are.

17

The Bottom Line on How to Get to the Top

There is no easy in education. What we do is difficult, challenging, perplexing, and rewarding. There also is no 'one best way' to do anything, or we would all already be doing it. However, there are clear differences between the most successful teachers in a school and those who continually struggle.

In every school we have highly effective teachers who connect with students every day. When we go into their classroom, it almost seems magical. They are smiling and upbeat, and the students are observant and engaged. We all want to be that teacher, and if we draw from their knowledge and practices, we can be.

There are certain teachers that students remember and always will feel connected to. We've had them during our own school career and your school does as well.

Some cynics like to say education is broken. I think a few actually wish it were. But as long as there are outstanding teachers, we can rest assured it is not broken. When you go into the best teacher in a school's classroom, you don't want to leave. They make every child feel important, and they make every student feel special. We had that teacher when we were young and we still remember their smile, their laugh, what they taught us, and how

DOI: 10.4324/9781003492535-21

we felt when they were around. They may have been that special person who inspired you to dedicate your life to making others' lives better.

We have two main ways to grow our schools. Add exceptional people and help those we currently have become exceptional. There really are no other options. Each action we take at the state, district, or building level should run through the filter of, *Will these things help us increase the quality and number of new people entering our schools and/or help increase the quality of the people we currently have?* If they will not, then we are probably focusing on the wrong things.

The Difference Is Talent

Great teachers are intelligent, caring, and have an incredible work ethic. They are team players and support individuals. They have gifts, and these gifts are all a talent. They are more talented than others, and they have a strong desire to share their gifts. Make sure you regularly reinforce them, value them, and stroke them. I've heard leaders say I don't pay much attention to my best teachers because they will be fine anyway. I promise you this: If they are just 'fine,' it is an incredible price to pay. We already have plenty of fine. What we need is *more great*. If you do not take care of your best teachers, then I promise, I guarantee, someone else will.

You have educators in your school who can connect with each student who crosses their doorway. They do it with the same budget as everyone else. They do it with the same superintendent as every teacher in the district. And they do it with the same population and community as everyone else. If they can do it, so can everyone else. We don't need to innovate. We need to replicate. All the teachers need to be like the best, so that all students can have the teacher they need and the teacher they deserve.

We really can get all the teachers in our schools to become more like the best teachers. We all know it and we need to start now.

References

Benigni, R. (1997). *Life is beautiful*. Cecchi Gori Distribuzione.

Berne, E. (1958). Transactional analysis: A new and effective method of group therapy. *American Journal of Psychotherapy*, *12*(4), 735–743.

Gonzalez, J. (2016). *How pineapple charts revolutionize professional development*. www.cultofpedagogy.com/pineapple-charts/

Murray, H. (2023). *Transactional analysis theory and therapy*. SimplyPsychology. www.simplypsychology.org/transactional-analysis-eric-berne.html

Whitaker, T. (2010). *Leading school change*. Routledge.

Whitaker, T. (2014). *Shifting the monkey: The art of protecting good people from liars, criers, and other slackers*. Solution Tree.

Whitaker, T. (2020a). *What great principals do differently: Twenty things that matter most* (3rd ed.). Routledge.

Whitaker, T. (2020b). *What great teachers do differently: Nineteen things that matter most* (3rd ed.). Routledge.

Whitaker, T., & Fiore, D. (2016a). *Dealing with difficult parents* (2nd ed.). Routledge.

Whitaker, T., & Fiore, D. (2016b). *A school leader's guide to dealing with difficult parents* (2nd ed.). Routledge.

Printed and bound by CPI Group (UK) Ltd, Croydon, CR0 4YY

06/11/2024

01784859-0011